Immigration and the Bible

a guide for radical welcome

BY JOAN M. MARUSKIN

Women's Division
The General Board of Global Ministries
The United Methodist Church

CONTENTS

PROLOGUE

The child stirred. His mother held her breath. He was a miracle, born in a cave, because there was no room in the inn. The light of a single star lit the child's face. He opened his eyes and she gasped silently. His eyes revealed the wisdom of the ages. In the depth of her being, she realized this was the promised child who came so that all might have life. At the same time, she was deeply saddened as she realized he was also a stranger in a strange land. Born on the move, he was destined to be on the move throughout his life.

He had come from God, of that she was certain, and he would return to God, but even more she knew that there was a mystical, magical connection between the child and God that was yet to be explained. She realized that he had been sent as a stranger in a strange land to show a path of radical, inclusive hospitality, acceptance, and hope to all people. He was born to be the stranger, the sojourner, and the alien in the land. In that role, he was also born to reach out to the other across all borders. She knew that his birth brought a new light to the world. The angel had said, "Peace on Earth. Good will to all."

Peace is possible, she thought, *and somehow this child holds the key to that peace.* Just then he looked deeply into her eyes. *He knows*, she realized, *he knows that he is the incarnation of all that she had been taught about scriptures.* She knew the ancient Hebrew narratives. She cherished the stories about the migrant God whose spirit moved across the waters at the time of creation. This was the same God who cared for and migrated with the people of the creation narrative and beyond. She was familiar with God's people, and they had all been on the move. The majority of God's people were poor and marginalized, just like her. They were migrants, refugees, immigrants, asylum seekers, widows, orphans, strangers, and outsiders. She had memorized the details of the stories of Adam and Eve, Abraham and his family, Noah, Joseph, Ruth and Boaz, the psalms, the prophets, and, of course, her ancestral nation's exodus. Her child was the incarnation of their hopes and even more so the incarnation of their God.

She worshipped and served a God who had cared for the people, traveled with the people, and taught the people the importance of caring for all of God's creation. While growing up she had often been reminded that God repeatedly stated the worship desired was care of the widows, the orphans, and the strangers. She was to never forget that they had once been strangers in a strange land. Her arms held the newest stranger, one destined not only to be a stranger but to be a refugee, an asylum seeker, and an undocumented migrant.

His would not be an easy life, but he would model for all a life lived with an open heart and an open mind, and he would open doors for the least, the last, and the lost. He was born as one of the marginalized. He would reach out to those even more marginalized. And, finally, he would chart a path for the ages. It was a big undertaking for so small a child. He opened his eyes again and smiled. Her heart melted. "Welcome, little stranger," she said. "Welcome, baby Jesus, welcome."

INTRODUCTION

T he Bible is the ultimate immigration handbook. It was written by, for, and about migrants, immigrants, refugees, and asylum seekers. It gives directions for responding to sisters and brothers from around the world who come to a land seeking safety, sanctuary, and sustenance. It is also the book that many of our ancestors used to help them survive the stress and strain of integrating into a new country. The Bible offers guidance and direction for persons who migrate or immigrate by choice and for persons who flee because of devastation and destruction from violence or natural disasters. It is the inspired word of the migrant God, the refugee Christ, and the Holy Spirit, who accompany us and every migrant, immigrant, refugee, and asylum seeker. Scriptures provide the basis for practicing a theology of radical, inclusive hospitality.

This text will provide an overview of the biblical narrative. It will highlight the migration narrative and compare the lives of our faith's ancestors with the lives of modern day migration narratives. In addition, United Methodist and other faith-based ministries that provide radical inclusive hospitality will be highlighted to enable the readers to see and model faith in action.

Theologically, the text will develop the need for and methods of practice that can be used to develop radical hospitality in response to the strangers in the twenty-first century. Radical hospitality is inclusive hospitality developed by embracing the unity of the diverse Trinity and the teachings of the Bible. God, the creator, repeatedly mandated hospitality to strangers in the Hebrew Bible.

Christ Jesus came as the refugee, migrant, stranger, sojourner, and asylum seeker, who modeled not only lifestyle but acceptance of and hospitality toward strangers without regard to religious, social, ethnic, or economic status. We believe that Christ is in us and that we are physical hosts to the migrant Christ. This hosting requires great diligence, as our actions may distort the image of the Christ in us. We are asking Jesus to participate in all of our actions. Also, the Holy Spirit moves and works with us to guide and direct our responses in the Kairos moment in which we live. *God comes to us as the stranger waiting for welcome.*

We are challenged to respond by living lives of radical hospitality and building hospitable communities that welcome all of God's people into our homes, our hearts, our minds, and our houses of worship. This challenge necessitates head knowledge of the contents of scripture and heart knowledge of the love of Christ that will enable us to act in love toward all God's people, and it demands a willingness to let the Holy Spirit into our lives. Throughout the scriptures there is a mandate to care for the stranger because caring for the stranger is caring for God and caring for ourselves. The early Christians embraced this concept and welcomed everyone.

This text is written to help contemporary followers of Christ do the following:

- Develop an understanding of the biblical narrative as a migration story.
- Develop a theology of radical, inclusive hospitality.
- Define the role of God, Son, and Holy Spirit in migration.
- Learn about ministries of radical inclusive hospitality.
- Grow spiritually as individuals and communities.

The early disciples realized, as do we, that in order to build truly hospitable communities, it is sometimes necessary to choose between following God's law or human law. This issue is addressed in the text, and the final chapter provides an overview of immigration law to aid in understanding complex, present-day immigration questions. There is some repetition in the text. This is to ensure that readers who study only selected chapters have key information.

The companion participant's guide consists of supplementary and liturgical resources, discussion questions, and activities for each chapter (and a separate leader's guide is available via the United Methodist Women website: www.unitedmethodistwomen.org). These studies are developed to assist participants in opening the borders of their minds, hearts, homes, and churches to Christ the stranger who comes to us as men, women, and children from around the world. The companion participant's guide also contains an appendix of materials to help in developing responses to the strangers in our land because once we were strangers and have been touched by Christ and asked to respond to immigrants, migrants, refugees, and asylum seekers with radical hospitality.

CHAPTER 1
The Call to Radical Hospitality

Then God said, "Let us make humankind
in our image, according to our likeness;
and let them have dominion over the fish of
the sea, and over the birds of the air,
and over the cattle, and over all the
wild animals of the earth, and over every
creeping thing that creeps upon the earth.
So God created humankind in his image,
in the image of God he created them;
male and female he created them."

—Genesis 1: 26–27

We the people of God are on a journey. It is a physical journey on earth as living images of God, who said in Genesis, "Let us make humankind in our own image: male and female," and in Matthew 25, "As you did it to the least of these, you did it to me." Wherever we are, whatever we are doing, and with whomever we are interacting, we must remember that we are each to the other, with no exception, the image of God.

In addition, we share a spiritual journey as we seek to live godly lives and plan and hope for life eternal with all God's people. Many of us see ourselves as strangers in this world on our way to eternal life in heaven. For this reason we identify with the strangers and include them in our journey. The stranger comes to teach us and give us the priceless gift of identity.

Many Christians forget this identity, and in doing so they open the door to justifying violence and wars that kill brothers and sisters who are also children of the living God. When we forget that we don't belong to a specific nationality or race as much as we belong to God and God's people, we fight to defend turf that isn't ours to defend. We give our greatest allegiance to temporary land and wealth and government, and to protect those things we disobey Jesus who says, "Love your enemies" (Matthew 5:44). When we believe ourselves to be exiles and aliens, then our greatest allegiance goes to God. This identity clarifies for us when we are to obey our temporary government and when we need a higher calling.[1]

A thorough study of scriptures makes it obvious that our journey is a communal migration story. We make our way to heaven reaching for the hand of God, who is reaching out to us, and we reach back with our other hand to hold the hands of other spiritual migrants, who are also walking the path to eternal life. The biblical mandate to care for the stranger because "once we were strangers in a strange land" was modeled and voiced by God. It has been affirmed by the life of the migrant, refugee Christ to whom we owe our salvation and is being confirmed and continued by the Holy Spirit who travels with us. We are all citizens of God's household.

Radical Hospitality

We are called to live lives of radical hospitality by welcoming all of God's people into our homes, our minds, our hearts, and our houses of worship. This call will necessitate head knowledge of scripture and heart knowledge of Christ's love that will enable us to act in love toward all. Scriptures mandate care of the stranger because doing so is caring for God and caring for ourselves as we move into wholeness.

On our journey, it is necessary to develop a new theology of radical hospitality that encompasses, welcomes, accepts, includes, and embraces all of God's people and creation. Its inclusivity sees all persons, documented and undocumented, as images of the living God and welcomes them not as strangers but as sisters and brothers. This inclusive hospitality also sees Jesus Christ as the center of a number of communities patterned after the community that is exemplified in the Holy Trinity of creating God, redeeming Son, and guiding Holy Spirit. Jesus welcomes all creation into that community. We develop this new theology by realizing that God gave instructions for responses to strangers in the Hebrew Bible through repeated mandates to care for them and to remember that once we were strangers in the land. Christ Jesus lived the life of a refugee and migrant. (Father Rene Castañeda, while working in the Altar, Sonora, area of Mexico, called Jesus "the Migrant Jesus" and said that God has given us the privilege of responding to "the Migrant Jesus.[2]") The Holy Spirit has been sent to travel with us and to guide and teach us in living lives that are pleasing to the God of the universe.

Amos Yong tells us,

> The redemptive economy of the triune God invites our participation as guests and hosts in the divine hospitality revealed in Christ by the power of the Holy Spirit. . . . As guests and hosts, sometimes simultaneously, we are obligated only to discern the Spirit's presence and activity so that we can perform the appropriate practices representing the hospitable God. Which tongues we speak and what practices we engage in will depend on where

we are, who we are interacting with, and what the social, political, and economic structures are that give shape to our encounter.[3]

Radical hospitality says to all, you are welcome, and we are ready to open our hearts and minds to include you as part of this community. This hospitality is modeled in the Benedictine's practice of inclusive hospitality and acceptance. "When we accept, we take an open stance to the other person. It is more than piously tolerating them. We stand in the same space and we appreciate who they are, right now at this moment, and affirm the Sacred in them."[4] It is also modeled in The United Methodist Church's call for radical, inclusive hospitality, welcoming everyone into Christ's community of love, and in its Rethink Church movement, which moves congregations out of their churches to meet the world at its points of greatest need.

On May 5, 2009, United Methodist bishops took Rethink Church to the streets with a workers outreach to day laborers. It called for the people of God to leave the pews and go into the streets as bearers of radical hospitality.

At Casa de Maryland, a community organization for immigrants in the Washington, DC, area, bishops gathered with day laborers to share communion and build community. "This was a day of taking the good news out into the world. United Methodists, look around you. There are so many opportunities to be the church day in and day out," said Bishop Minerva Carcaño of the Desert Southwest Conference of The United Methodist Church and chairperson of the denomination's immigration task force. "It is a joy to be Christ's presence in the world."

Casa de Maryland was started by the Rev. David Rocha, a former day laborer who fled persecution in Colombia. He was once denied a cup of coffee by a church, and so he began serving coffee, providing scriptures, and praying with day workers in a parking lot. "A cup of hot coffee is the equivalent of a cup of cold water in the Hebrew Bible," Mr. Rocha said. "It can say, I care about you. I am your friend."

Mr. Rocha is the chairperson of Hispanic and Latino ministries for the Baltimore-Washington Conference of The United Methodist Church. The blessings his ministry has brought to the greater church demonstrate the value of being a laborer in God's vineyard. He believes we are to "leave the four walls. Go out. The church is very alive. If we keep our pews full, the people in the streets will not find Jesus." *From "Bishops Launch Rethink Church with Worker Outreach" by Linda Green for United Methodist News Service, May 5, 2009 (www.umcom.org).*

Creating Hospitable Communities

This communal pattern of openness demonstrates that although we seek eternal life in God's Kin-dom* and God's Kin-dom is within us, we live in God's community on earth and should seek to build inclusive communities mirroring Christ's openness to all. The Hebrews lived in community. Jesus moved and lived in community with a large base of very inclusive male and female followers. The Holy Spirit was first sent at Pentecost to an incredibly diverse community. The early Christians lived in community. In seeking to develop a Christ-centered community free of fear of the other, it is necessary

---

* "Kin-dom" is a term popularized by Drew University ethics professor Ada Maria Isasi-Diaz.

to concentrate on developing a community that is composed of the citizens of this land, Jesus the Christ, and the strangers who reside in this land, without regard to whether they have "documents."

Just as the Trinity is composed of the creating God, redeeming Son, and guiding Holy Spirit, all communities are models of a communal relationship that varies with time and occasion. In relationship to immigrants, refugees, and migrants, it is possible to live in a number of communities. These communities would all be composed of various groupings of citizens and strangers with Jesus Christ as their center. Some communities would have a combination of members. However, all communities would have Christ as the center. Within each community, the individual members would work to see Christ standing between them and the strangers with whom they are working. (Whenever Christ is recognized as present in an interaction among people, the interaction becomes more loving and caring.) With Christ as the center, all communities live in a covenantal relationship guided and directed by Christ's love.

A community practicing radical hospitality focuses on Christ and Christ's creative life of hospitality and inclusivity. It asks all persons to lead lives of love, truth, and goodness by purposefully expanding the borders of their hearts, minds, homes, and churches by opening their hearts, minds, and doors. It recognizes Christ as the breaking in of God and the freeing of all persons from past demons and divisions. It is a theology of sharing one another's crosses instead of bearing our own crosses. "Bear one another's burdens, and in this way you will fulfill the law of Christ" (Galatians 6:2). The model for cross sharing and bearing is seen in the life of Christ who was helped in carrying his cross by Simon of Cyrene. This is a key example of a cross-sharing relationship. This willingness to carry one another's crosses will be an active theology of following in the footsteps of Jesus who came not to be served but to serve, who crossed many cultural and religious borders, and who carried the crosses of the whole world.

In Mark 8:34, Jesus called the crowd, who had gathered with his disciples, and said to them, "If any want to become my followers, let them deny themselves and take up their cross and follow me." Note that the first instruction is to "deny themselves" and then to "take up their cross and follow." Each person is to give up self-concern and to carry the cross of another. In doing so, we suddenly discover that there is another person carrying our cross. That is one of the great blessings of radical, inclusive hospitality. The hosts and hostesses discover that they are receiving the greatest blessings as their lives expand and change in ways they never imagined. Whenever we open up to another there is growth.

The Milwaukee Native American Ministry United Methodist Church is a small storefront mission church in the heart of Milwaukee, Wisconsin. It has an occupancy permit for ninety-nine people. In December 2006, Pastor Rob Odum was praying for the direction of the church in the coming year. While praying, he heard the still small voice of God say, "Write this down: next year there will be a 65 percent increase in the congregation." After pondering those words for a few minutes, he wrote them down and continued to pray.

On a cold and snowy Sunday morning in January 2007, as worship was starting, Mr. Odum looked out and saw a crowd of Burmese refugees, in their traditional Karen clothing, walking through the front door. Although most spoke no English, they had come to worship and join the Native American congregation. At that moment, radical, inclusive hospitality based on welcoming the stranger according to biblical and Native American traditions began.

The group of Karen refugees from Burma smiled and laughed as they entered the church. Beusie, a tiny grandmother who along with her husband was a spiritual leader of the group, announced that this was the church they were going to attend. Although there were three pastors in their group, they came to church faithfully and offered the small, aging church congregation new and unexpected opportunities to become a church in mission rather than a mission church. There were Karen children and teens, so vacation Bible school and teens helping to lead worship became a reality.

Eventually worship was split into two services, one in English the other in Karen. After the Karen congregation outgrew the size of the storefront church they moved on to partner with a Hmong United Methodist Church in Milwaukee. But not before the Burmese refugees, concerned about the homeless white and African-American population in their area, began providing food to the homeless and hungry in their neighborhood. United Methodist radical hospitality of open hearts, open minds, and open doors welcomed the strangers and were blessed by Christ among them as the center of a new radically inclusive community. *From personal communication with Rob Odum, Native American Ministry United Methodist Church, Milwaukee, Wisconsin. Used with permission.*

Persons who practice this new level of hospitality seek freedom for all. They have heard God say, "I have observed the misery of my people who are in Egypt; I have heard their cry. I will send you to Pharaoh to bring my people out of Egypt. I will be with you" (Exodus 3:7, 10, 12). The words "I will be with you" are key to this theology, which affirms that God is present in all things and with all people. God does not prefer one group of people over another. Each and every person has been created in God's image. To reject any human is to reject God.

Radical hospitality springs from an active rather than passive theology. It is a lived-out theology of the people and requires a grassroots movement to sustain and spread its growth. It will grow through hands-on ministry to the uprooted strangers, who are most in need. Its practitioners remember that Jesus Christ got his hands dirty as he lived and moved among the suffering of the world. They truly believe, as Christ did, that no one is untouchable. We are called to respond and "be doers of the word, and not merely hearers who deceive themselves"(James 1:22).

Just as Jesus offered living water to the Samaritan woman at the well, Humane Borders fills 100 barrels of water a week in the Arizona desert to offer water to save the lives of migrants crossing the U.S.–Mexico border. A cup of water says, "We care." A cup of water can be the difference between life and death in a desert where the temperatures can reach 160 degrees. Since the 1990s at least one person per day has died after crossing the border. Humane Borders (www.humaneborders.org) is a collaboration of more than 70 public, private, and faith-based organizations including many United Methodist Churches, bishops, and Methodists for Social Action. Its sole mission is to take death out of migration. Its members preach the gospel through their actions with this life-saving mission.[5]

Theology of Acceptance

This active theology is a theology of acceptance of all people. To accept means to embrace other human beings exactly as they are. In many cases, rather than acceptance, tolerance of the other is taught. It is crucial to realize that to tolerate means to allow without prohibiting or opposing, to recognize and respect, and/or to put up with. There is a great difference between acceptance and tolerance.

It is important, as we consider radical hospitality, to recognize that the operative word is *acceptance*. We are called to accept one another because through acceptance, love is possible. We love those whom we accept. We rarely love those whom we tolerate. Radical hospitality means welcoming every person without regard to social, economic, ethnic, educational, religious, emotional, or immigration status.

All humanity is called to accept the present, analyze the past, acknowledge responsibility, and actively participate in the formation of an inclusive future. The past has caused many divisions and much pain among diverse groups. Some of those wounds are still open, and many scars remain. These divisions are greatest among ethnic and socioeconomic groups. These divisions are also visible in the churches, which continue to be among the most segregated organizations. Martin Luther King Jr.'s mid-twentieth-century lament that Sunday morning was the most segregated time of the week continues to remain a sad truth. Therefore, the church must recognize its intended or unintended responsibility for exclusivity and accept responsibility for past history and vow to change future history. We do this by actively working to build welcoming communities that accept and embrace everyone. This means we must recognize that divisions exist and that we have helped them to become institutionalized. We must look at ourselves, our churches, our communities, and our country, and if there are persons we do not fully accept, we must confess our sin of exclusivity, repent, follow Jesus' advice to go and sin no more (John 8:11) and open the doors of our churches and go into the streets inviting all to the banquet.

West Nashville United Methodist Church in West Nashville, Tennessee, was a declining, predominately white middle-class congregation. The neighborhood included people living on the margins, a growing Latino population, and numerous transients. The congregation decided to embrace its diverse community; they sold the parsonage and invested the money in neighborhood ministries.

A bilingual English/Spanish worship service has been developed. The liturgy and bulletins are projected in and printed in both languages with simultaneous translation. Every few months the whole service is in Spanish with the translation for English speakers. The sermon translation is not word for word but dynamic, with a focus on the life needs of the Hispanic members who come from multiple countries.

The music selections in worship are in both languages. Sometimes the verses alternate languages, but most often people sing in their first language. The choir has learned Spanish pronunciation in order to lead equally in both languages. Worship leaders get the Pentecost effect of hearing the mix of languages simultaneously. Amanda Bachus, who attends the church and edits *El Interprete* states, "Having our worship together makes us understand that as children of God we are one in Christ."

West Nashville United Methodist Church sought partnerships to expand its outreach. The church began offering English as a second language (ESL) classes, providing a place for AARP volunteers to prepare free tax returns for older adults and low-income persons, providing Alcoholics Anonymous meeting space, and opening a food bank. Each week church members (and volunteers from other United Methodist churches) provide a free community meal. Vacation Bible school and the addition of Latino celebrations have brought more families into the church.

The congregation's identity is "Two Languages, Many Cultures, One Gospel." The diversity of the church has also attracted nonimmigrant young families and singles who appreciate the multicultural environment and community outreach. *From personal communication with United Methodist Communications staff and West Nashville United Methodist Church congregation member Crys Zinkiewicz. Used with her permission.*

Prayer and Scriptures

A first step in transitioning into a radically hospitable congregation is to pray. We can begin with a very simple prayer that can result in monumental growth. Very simply, as an individual and in community, pray that God will change us according to God's plan. "Change me, God. Change me, according to your plan." And "Change us, God. Change us, according to your plan." Note that we do not give God any instructions. We simply pray that change happens according to God's plan because we know that God has plans for all and has given us instructions on caring for the strangers in our midst. When we give control to God our lives change for the better.

This prayer can be most effective in any life situation, as not one of us has the power to change another being. We can only change ourselves. Praying to change according to God's will has the potential to bring peace and harmony in any situation and will result in amazing events and changes. Each time we let go and give God control, we become ever more who we were created to be. We become instruments of God enabling others to also become the people they were created to be. As United Methodists, we can help enhance and develop our theology by following John Wesley's quadrilateral of scripture, reason, tradition, and experience.

Scripture is of primary importance. We understand and respond to scripture through studying the history and practices of the church, interpreting it sensibly with rational thinking and embracing it with our personal and communal journey in Christ.

Looking to scriptures, we know that the Bible was written by the people of God who began the development of our holy scriptures as their oral histories were shared and passed around campfires through memorized words, song, music, and dance. They shared God's word as they migrated to new lands following commands and directions given to them by God.

As writing developed, the memorized stories were written down and passed on from generation to generation. The earliest writings date back to about 3500 BCE and are credited to the Phoenicians. Their writing was the basis for Aramaic, the ancient language of Syria. It, in turn, was the basis for the Hebrew written language. By the twenty-second century BCE, the people of God had long been on the move carrying their spoken histories with them. Written language assured the preservation of the narratives, which gave humanity both God's instructions for living and the history of the God's people.

Over the centuries the scriptures came from different migrant groups and were brought together and codified by the early church councils as the Holy Scriptures. The Bible has become the definitive word about and for the people of the God of Abraham, who became the believers known as the Jews and the Christians. They are the principal people in both the Hebrew Bible/Old Testament and the New Testament. They have been and continue to be on the move throughout history, the world, and into the future

Islam is the third Abrahamic religion with its roots in the birth of Ishmael, the first son of Abraham, the descendants of whom God promised to make into a great nation. Jews, Christians, and Muslims all honor and share the same religious patriarchs. The

Koran also contains many of the same narratives as the Bible and instructions on welcoming the stranger.

Radical hospitality embraces the strangers who are people without a permanent place and a welcoming community. It accepts them and offers them that place and community.

> To be without a place means to be detached from the basic, life-supporting institutions—family, work, polity, religious community, and to be without networks of relations that sustain and support human beings. People without a place who are also without financial resources are the most vulnerable people. This is the condition in which homeless people, displaced poor people, refugees, and undocumented persons find themselves. . . . Through most of its history, the Christian hospitality tradition has expressed a normative concern for strangers who could not provide for or defend themselves.[6]

Building Hospitable Communities

The mandate to lovingly care for the stranger continues today. Any action not taken in love is an action not blessed by the living, loving God. Denying any person access to God's community is an action that rejects God from the community of saints because God appears to us in many forms and may be the stranger knocking at our door. The early followers of Christ were known as the people of The Way. They were a community of saints called to follow Christ's teachings and to be his hands and feet in the world. They viewed themselves as an open community and welcomed all classes and ethnic groups.

Henri Nouwen reminds us that "to follow Christ means to relate to each other with the mind of Christ; that is, to relate to each other as Christ did to us in servanthood and humility."[7] He explains that as we discover one another as travelers on the same path a new community is formed and is based in compassion, which is inseparable from community. It is that compassion that energizes and drives disciples following Christ. The people of The Way embraced their sainthood and sought to embrace one another. This is epitomized in Paul's calling the church community the body of Christ. It is a compliment to its members and a challenge to the way Christians live their lives.

Somewhere along the line, it became much more popular for Christians to call ourselves a community of sinners and focus on our sinful side rather than on our saintly side. How can we be the body of Christ and identify ourselves as sinners? It is time to rethink this language and realize that Jesus called his followers not to be sinners but to be saints, as we were instructed by Jesus in Matthew 5:43–48.

> You have heard that it was said, "You shall love your neighbor and hate your enemy." But I say to you, Love your enemies and pray for those who persecute you, so that you may be children of your Father in heaven; for he makes his sun rise on the evil and on the good, and sends rain on the righteous and on the unrighteous. For if you love those who love you, what reward do you have? Do not even the tax collectors do the same? And if you greet only your brothers and sisters, what more are you doing than others? Do not even the Gentiles do the same? Be perfect, therefore, as you're heavenly Father is perfect.

To be perfect is to love perfectly. It is to love as God loves, and "God loves beyond our dreams, extravagantly, without limit."[8] We are to love all people, including those considered to be outsiders or enemies. To be a community of saints is to be a radically hospitable community. The purpose of this book is to provide a biblically sound theological and spiritual basis for developing open, welcoming, hospitable communities that embrace all of God's children without regard to their immigration, economic, social, religious, emotional, or ethnic status.

Christ instructs us to love as God loves and thereby be perfect as God in heaven is perfect (Matthew 5:48). As United Methodists we know and understand that we are moving on to perfection. What would our lives be like if churches in the twenty-first century taught its members that they were saints rather than sinners? How would your self-image change if you thought of yourself as a saint (which is Christ's intent for you) rather than a sinner?

In John 12:46, Jesus states, "I have come as light into the world, that everyone who believes in me may not remain in darkness." To live a life of a sinner is to live in darkness. To live as a saint is to bring light to the world. By following and living according to the words of the Light of the World, we are able to turn away from sin. We do this by following Jesus as our teacher, brother, savior, and friend. We have the option to be a saint or a sinner. Jesus saw us as saints.

Jesus is our teacher, just as he was the teacher of the disciples. Verses that verify this and demonstrate Christ's plan for all of us can be found in John 13:12–14:

> After he had washed their feet, had put on his robe, and had returned to the table, he said to them, "Do you know what I have done to you? You call me Teacher and Lord— and you are right, for that is what I am. So if I, your Lord and Teacher, have washed your feet, you also ought to wash one another's feet."

When did we last wash someone's feet? The question for the church is why is this action of Jesus not one of the sacraments? And, finally, why is washing another's feet avoided instead of welcomed?

Christ welcomed the opportunity and instructed his disciples to do likewise. Jesus was very specific about having come to serve. Titus 2:14 reads, "He it is who gave himself for us that he might redeem us from all iniquity and purify for himself a people of his own who are zealous for good deeds." (This is a far cry from contemporary thought of a people who are sinners in need of being saved.)

In Matthew 20:26b–28 Jesus calls his disciples and says, "Whoever wishes to be first among you must be your slave; just as the Son of Man came not to be served but to serve, and to give his life a ransom for many." This theme of service and sacrifice runs throughout the scriptures as a basis for eternal life.

Where would the Christian church be if we had embraced the concept of being a community of blessed saints rather than a community of fallen sinners? Potentially, we would be more open and welcoming. We would be sharing more and having less (which might be one of the reasons being a community of sinners is preferable to being a community of saints). To offer radical hospitality means to share what we have. The early believers took Jesus literally, called themselves saints, and followed his instructions in Matthew 19:21, where the young man asked Jesus what he must do in addition to following the commandments to have eternal life and Jesus said, "If you wish to be perfect, go, sell your possessions, and give the money to the poor, and you will have treasure in heaven; then come, follow me." (Note: He is not told to simply believe in Jesus but to come and follow Jesus.)

This is a difficult order to ponder. Many of the early saints willingly sold their possessions and shared what they had in common with one another and strangers. However, very few translations of scripture tell the young man to sell "all" he has. The majority say to "sell your possessions" without the word "all." We know that the disciples maintained the basic necessities of life; they had families and houses. Mark 2:1 states that Jesus had a home in Capernaum.

We do not know if the rich young man eventually followed Jesus, but we do know he went away sad. We also know that Jesus said it is harder for a rich man to get to heaven than for a camel to go through the eye of a needle. He also said that with God all things are possible. Perhaps the key is how much do we need for basic existence and at what point does the accumulation of stuff get in the way of our relationship with God? Perhaps before purchasing anything we should begin to ask ourselves, do I need this, or do I want it? Fulfilling needs is very different from fulfilling wants.

In Luke 12:15, Jesus warned about accumulating more than was necessary, he cautioned, "Take care! Be on your guard against all kinds of greed; for one's life does not consist in the abundance of possessions." If the pursuit of "stuff," caring for "stuff," and storing "stuff" takes more time than our time spent serving God, there is very possibly a stuff problem in our lives. A house full of stuff is not an insurance policy for eternal life.

After Christ's resurrection and before they were called Christians, his followers began developing house churches, praying in cell groups, welcoming strangers, being taught by people with social status and by those who were slaves, and sharing communal meals as equals. They were companions—the literal translation of the Latin word for companion means to "break bread" together. Food is powerful, sharing meals says you belong here, which helps to explain the power in the Eucharist.[9]

Migration Statistics

Perhaps the instruction to sell possessions is an admonition to simplify and share what we have so all might have enough to live with similar sustaining lifestyles. God's world has the resources to supply the basic necessities of a simple lifestyle for all. The developed world, especially the United States and Western Europe, of which the United States is the largest manufacturer and consumer, uses 60 percent of the world's goods. However, it contains only 12 percent of the earth's population.[10] We seek the best bargains without regard to how, where, and by whom the goods are manufactured or harvested.

When we look at economies honestly, we see glaring gaps between the haves and the have nots. Poverty is rampant, everywhere, even in the United States. As a result, men, women, and children from countries whose economies cannot support them are forced to migrate across international borders in attempts to survive. Migrants are on the move across the world. If we compare the European and North American continents, they have landmasses of similar size. However, Europe hosts the largest number of immigrants, both documented and undocumented. The State of the World Population for the United Nations World Population 2006 Report indicated that 33 percent of the world's immigrants go to Western Europe, 20 percent to the United States, 7 percent to Russia, 4 percent to India, 3 percent to Canada, and the rest are scattered across the world.

The very poor are considered economic migrants and are not welcomed in the lands they enter. However, their labor is wanted at lower than minimum-wage levels and in jobs that most often citizens do not want. Although many people feel that everyone wants to come to the United States, across the globe people in need migrate to the nearest developed country. Migration is a worldwide phenomenon. In Europe there are an estimated six to fifteen million undocumented migrants. Also, in seventy countries, at least 10 percent of the population is immigrants.[11]

Immigration Terminology

In responding to immigrants by using the Bible as the ultimate immigration handbook, it is important to understand the terminology that is used in referring to sisters and brothers uprooted by choice or by chance. (A list of terms can be found in the appendix of the participant's guide.) Key identification terms are *emigrant, immigrant, migrant, refugee,* and *asylum seeker.* Contemporary terminology adds *documented* and *undocumented, authorized* and *unauthorized,* and *legal* and *illegal.* A person who leaves a country by choice for a new land is an emigrant. On entering that new country, he or she is an immigrant. *Immigrant* is often used as a general term to refer to anyone who was born in another land. It, as well as the word *stranger,* will be used in this text as a contemporary inclusive term. At times, the terms *documented* and *undocumented* will be used to identify immigration status. However, at times a more specific term will be used to define specific types of immigrants.

In the Bible, *stranger* is used as a synonym for the following terms: foreigner, stranger, alien, sojourner, immigrant, migrant, refugee, and asylum seeker. Contemporary language and immigration laws have increased the number of possible translations of the ancient word. In the twenty-first century, United Methodists, as well as most people of faith, prefer using the terms *stranger* or *sojourner* rather than *foreigner* or *alien.* However, to be biblically accurate, this text will use the New Revised Standard Version of the Bible for all quoted Bible passages. Readers are invited to consider each passage while reading and to decide which term (stranger or sojourner) would be their preferred contemporary term.

There are a variety of nuances to the status of persons in these categories. In the Hebrew Bible, they are referred to as strangers, aliens, sojourners, or foreigners. The term varies from translation to translation. Throughout this study, the term *stranger* will be used predominantly, as it is the term that is used, with very few variations, in a key hospitality passage in the New Testament, Hebrews 13:2: "Do not neglect to show hospitality to strangers, for by doing that some have entertained angels without knowing it." Keep in mind that stranger, at that time, specifically referred to a person from another land or area, not simply someone from the same town who had not been encountered before. (That is not to say that these persons should not also be welcomed, but for the sake of this discussion, a stranger is someone who has crossed a border.) At other times, a more definitive term will be used such as *migrant, immigrant, refugee,* or *asylum seeker.*

To be a migrant is to be on the move within the borders of a country or across international borders. Most migrants move to meet basic needs or to improve their present quality of life. Very often they travel for employment opportunities. Many who are seasonally employed would greatly prefer to go home at the season's end to be with their families. Any person who has moved from his or her home to another place has migrated. It is estimated that the average person moves twelve times in his or her life.

John Wesley was very often on the move. On February 6, 1736, he landed in Georgia as a missionary and the third minister of the established church in the American colonies. He preached to the scattered settlements traveling by boat and over Indian trails. In 1737, after differences with his parishioners, Wesley shook the dust off his feet and left Georgia and went home, "Having preached the gospel not as I ought but as I was able for one year and nearly nine months."[12] According to *The New Schaff-Herzog Encyclopedia of Religious Knowledge,* Volume XII, he is believed to have traveled in the course of his itinerant ministry more than 250,000 miles and to have preached more than 40,000 times. He introduced the itinerant ministry into the early Methodist societies, and when he died there were 541 itinerant ministers spreading the gospel as Methodists.

There are also migrants who are continually on the move. An example would be migrant workers, who follow the crops and bring in the harvests so all might eat. The Hebrew Bible instructs the growers to leave the gleanings for the migrants, who are strangers in their midst. Ruth was such a migrant, as was Joseph's family. We will read more about the biblical migrants throughout this text.

Refugees and asylum seekers are persons who are forced to flee their homelands because of persecution or credible fear of persecution because of their race, ethnicity, religion, membership in a particular social group, or political opinion. Refugees leave their home country and enter a country of first asylum. This is a place where they will be safe. There they must be identified as a refugee before they can move from that country to a permanent resettlement site.

In 2010, according to the United Nations High Commissioner for Refugees, there were an estimated 15.4 million refugees across the world.[13] Less than one percent of the world's refugees are permanently resettled. The majority are refugees (without full citizenship rights) for the rest of their lives unless the situation in their country of origin improves and they can return home. An asylum seeker flees to a safe country and applies for asylum, which means he or she has the burden of proving persecution or a credible fear of persecution on return. If the asylum claim is believed, the asylum seeker is granted refugee status in the country of asylum and he or she is permitted to stay.

Another popular current term is *illegal alien*. This is a person who has entered the country without proper documents and who does not have "permission" to be there. There appears to be general agreement both ecumenically and secularly that this has become a very derogatory term. First, God created every one of us, so in our Creator's eyes, no one is illegal. Second, the term *alien* has an additional and much different meaning than it did in biblical times. It means a very strange being from outer space as well as a person from another country. Therefore, the preferred terms are undocumented or unauthorized migrant, immigrant or person. However, the media, the government, and others continue to use the term *illegal alien* to mean an undocumented person.

Entering a country without documents is not a criminal act. It is a civil offense. Some immigration attorneys describe being undocumented as the equivalent of driving without a driver's license. Others feel that to enter a country without documents is unforgivable and should not be allowed. It is also important to note that almost half of the undocumented persons in this country came here legally. Initially, they had the proper paperwork to enter as tourists, students, or temporary workers. When their time limits were up, they did not return to their home country. There are many professionals in the country who are undocumented. There are also many undocumented Canadians and Europeans; however, because of their socioeconomic status or physical appearance they are rarely thought of as being undocumented.

One of my most embarrassing moments took place when I made the mistake of asking a Canadian national and well-known businessman, who was visiting with friends, if he was documented. The moment the question was asked, I regretted it. There was an awkward pause, which immediately told me the truth. This well-dressed, blond-haired, blue-eyed Canadian was undocumented. He had lived here for years and was never questioned. I should not have crossed that line. My home was no longer a safe haven for the stranger among us.

The Church of the Brethren teaches that "God made people. People made borders." First consider "God made people." We are the children of Adam and Eve, who were blessed by God to multiply, and they did. As we discuss language and terminology, the word *race* refers to the human race. There is biblically and scientifically only one race. On this point there is general consensus, although in practice we assign races according to color and features. Therefore, throughout this text the terms *ethnic group or ethnicity* will be used unless it is necessary to use race for historical accuracy. We are all members of a particular ethnic group, and we are all members of the human race.

Second, consider that people made borders. Borders are everywhere, including in our hearts, minds, homes, and churches. There are personal borders, local borders, regional borders, state borders, national borders, and institutional borders. We are followers of Christ, who was a migrant, an asylum seeker, a refugee, and undocumented. He began his adult life as a teacher/rabbi by quoting the following words from Isaiah in Luke 4:18–19: "The Spirit of the Lord is upon me, because he has anointed me to bring good news to the poor. He has sent me to proclaim release to the captives and recovery of sight to the blind, to let the oppressed go free, to proclaim the year of the Lord's favor." Jesus was the living proclamation of the Lord's favor. As his disciples we are called to live lives proclaiming the Lord's favor as well. As United Methodists, we are called to have open hearts, open minds, and open doors. Wherever we are, whatever we are doing, and with whomever we are interacting, we must remember that we are each to the other the image of God.

As we begin this study on immigration and the Bible, we ask, how open are our hearts, minds, and doors and those of our churches, families, friends, and communities? Let us covenant with one another to pray, "Change us, God. Change us according to your divine will."

Notes

1. Michelle Hershberger, A Christian View of Hospitality: Expecting Surprises (Scottsdale, PA: Herald Press, 1999), 215.
2. Rick Ufford-Chase, "Seeking God's Justice for People on the Move," Church & Society Presbyterian Magazine 95, no. 6 (2005): 5.
3. Amos Yong, Hospitality & the Other: Pentecost, Christian Practices and the Neighbor (Maryknoll, NY: Orbis Books, 2008), 127.
4. Daniel Homan and Lonni Collins Pratt, Radical Hospitality: Benedict's Way of Love (Brewster, MA: Paraclete Press, 2002), xxvi.
5. Mary Beth Coudal, "Humane Borders," Global Ministries, September 15, 2010, http://gbgm-umc.org/global_news/full_article.cfm?articleid=5846.

6. Christine D. Pohl, *Making Room: Recovering Hospitality as a Christian Tradition* (Grand Rapids, MI: Wm. B. Eerdmans, 1999), 87.

7. Henri J.M. Nouwen, *The Only Necessary Thing: Living a Prayerful Life* (New York: The Crossroad Publishing Company, 1999), 129.

8. Roberta Bondi, *To Love as God Loves: Conversations with the Early Church* (Minneapolis: Fortress Press, 1991), 101.

9. Homan and Pratt, *Radical Hospitality*, 115.

10. World Watch Institute, "The State of Consumption Today," October 18, 2011, www.worldwatch.org/node/810.

11. Eric Weiner and Lindsay Mangum, "Debunking Global Migration Myths," National Public Radio, June 6, 2007, www.npr.org/templates/story/story.php?storyId=10767136.

12. John Wesley, "John Wesley's Journals (Abridged)," www.revival-library.org/catalogues/1725ff/wesley.html.

13. Shiv Malik, "UNHCR Report Says Refugee Numbers at 15-Year High," *The Guardian*, June 19, 2011, www.guardian.co.uk/world/2011/jun/20/unhcr-report-refugee-numbers-15-year-high.

Chapter 2
The Biblical Migration Story

In the beginning when God created
the heavens and the earth, the earth was a formless
void and darkness covered the face of the deep, while
a wind from God swept over the face of the waters.

—Genesis 1:1–2

T he Bible begins with the migration of God's Spirit and ends with
John in exile on the Isle of Patmos writing of the New Jerusalem
coming down from heaven to earth. Between those two events, the
uprooted people of God migrate. They seek safety, sanctuary, and refuge, and God gives directions for welcoming the stranger and becomes
the stranger among and with them. Given these characteristics, one
would be inclined to think that what we have here is the text of a
sermon or exhortation. But such an easy classification is thwarted by
the clear declaration both at the beginning of the document (1 John
1:4) and at the end (1 John 5:13) that the author is writing.

In the beginning, all was darkness and void, and the Spirit of God
moved (migrated) over the face of the chaos (Genesis 1:1). The
Bible opens with God's Spirit (Ruah) migrating over the face of the
water, followed by God the Creator, who, after bringing into being
birds, fish, and animals (all of which migrate), moved throughout
creation looking for a caretaker for this world. Not finding one, God

said, "Let us create humankind in our image"(Genesis 1:26). God then created Adam and Eve in God's own image and gave them dominion over all the earth and told them to multiply and fill the earth. At that point, human migration began and continues as God's people of many colors and faiths continue to move, to migrate, to multiply, and to maintain the earth.

Today, as then, migration happens by choice when people decide to move for a variety of personal reasons: jobs, ministries, homes, family, relationships, or desires. It happens by chance when people are impacted by life circumstances, natural or economic disasters, violence, wars, and persecution or fear of persecution. We each have a personal migration story that adds to the biblical human migration story.

We are all part of God's plan of migration. The great majorities of people have either lived out a migration story or can trace their roots back to ancestors traveling from one place to another. In fact, if we embrace Adam and Eve as our original ancestors, we are all migrants in a strange land and very far from home. Genetically, we all go back to one man and one woman in Africa. This is generally accepted as both a biblical and scientific fact.

We all are, or have been, migrants, immigrants, refugees, or asylum seekers and at times both documented and undocumented. As believers in the God of Abraham, we trace our roots back to the Garden of Eden located in the area of four rivers: Pishon, Gihon, Tigris, and Euphrates. The exact location of the garden is unknown, but the text says the Gihon flows around the land of Cush (now known as Ethiopia) and the Tigris is east of Assyria. The other river is the Euphrates. Using biblical data, the Garden of Eden is thought to have been in either Ethiopia or Iraq. If we live in the Western World, we are a long way from home and living in lands that were unknown in biblical times.

Hebrew Bible and Migration

The Hebrew Bible (Old Testament), the New Testament, and post–New Testament times parallel the Trinity (God, Jesus, and Holy Spirit) through the development of a migration narrative and a biblical response to immigrants. In the Hebrew Bible, God modeled radical hospitality toward migrants and traveled with them as with all people. In the New Testament, Jesus came as a stranger, refugee, asylum seeker, migrant, and undocumented person. He lived an all-encompassing life of hope, peace, and love that demonstrated radical, inclusive hospitality to all including enemies. During his time on earth, Jesus was one with the other and demonstrated how to respond to the other in love. To culminate his teachings, Jesus sent the Holy Spirit to be with us and guide us and teach us as we struggle to live lives as Christ's disciples.

In the Hebrew Bible, more than three dozen times God mandates three categories of people to treat with great love, kindness, and respect. They are the widow, the orphan, and the stranger. Most churches embrace the mandate to care for the widows and the orphans. However, a much smaller number of churches embrace the mandate to care for the stranger. We tend to forget that we were once strangers in this strange land. Therefore, we are, according to scripture, required to embrace the stranger. In fact, in Genesis, Exodus, Leviticus, Deuteronomy, and other books of the Bible we are repeatedly told to treat them as one of us. These will be discussed throughout this text.

God modeled radical hospitality by clothing Adam and Eve before they were sent into exile. Next he put a mark of protection on Cain who had killed his brother and was sent from the garden as a fugitive.

Just about everyone migrated in the Hebrew Bible. A natural disaster caused Noah and family to migrate. Abram and Sarai migrated when told to by God. They did not go alone. God was with them and appeared under the trees at Mamre.

Moses became perhaps the first recorded undocumented minor when he was set adrift in a basket in the river. Saved by Pharaoh's daughter, he grew up to rail against injustice, kill an Egyptian, flee for safety, and eventually return to lead the people of God out of Egypt and toward the Promised Land and new and better lives.

An undocumented migrant once reminded me that it is easy to compare the plight of the undocumented workers in the United States with the Hebrews. He wondered what would happen if all the workers without documents were to leave. It is a serious question, as the almost 11 million undocumented persons are integrated into the lives of at least 50 million American families, are 5 percent of the work force, perhaps 50 percent of our agricultural workers, 29 percent of our roofers, and the list goes on. If they would leave, our family and economic structure would be severely devastated. It is estimated that legalizing them would over 10 years add $1.5 trillion to our GDP.[1]

New York City is a prime example of a city of immigrants. Its three million immigrants make up 40 percent of the population. It is estimated that 500,000 of them are undocumented. In a Senate testimony, Mayor Michael Bloomberg in 2006 stated, "Although they broke the law by illegally crossing our borders or overstaying their visas, our city's economy would be a shell of itself had they not, and it would collapse if there were deported. The same holds true for the nation."[2]

Scriptures provide God's mandate to care for the strangers. Hearing calls for massive deportations, we might ask: Are we one with the strangers of the Hebrew Bible or are our actions much closer to those of Pharaoh and his court? In *No Man Is an Island*, Thomas Merton reminds us, "Every person becomes the image of the God they adore."

In the Hebrew Bible, God was with the Hebrews as they migrated, first as a cloud by day and a pillar of fire by night, later in the Ark of the Covenant. Eventually, the Hebrews reached the Promised Land

and entered Canaan. We rejoice at their victory, but it is important to realize that whenever a people are conquered, there are refugees and displaced people who have lost their homes, their livelihood, and many of their loved ones. The uprooting of the Canaanites is an example of one of the texts of violence in the Hebrew Bible and gives us a context for understanding why Jesus came to bring peace to the world.

The many wars in the Bible resulted in death, destruction, and devastation being a way of life for the Hebrews. Throughout that turmoil, God sent prophets to warn, travel with, and admonish the people. Isaiah, Jeremiah, Daniel, and Ezekiel all went into exile and all spoke God's word to ears that were very often closed to what God was saying.

New Testament and Migration

In the New Testament, God sent Jesus, as a migrant and refugee, to give the people another chance to respond and follow instructions. There is a wonderful praise song that begins, "He came from heaven to earth. . . . " Jesus migrated to earth to live with us and among us being both fully human and fully God.

According to tradition, Mary and Joseph were migrating to their place of origin for a tax roll count. Jesus was born in a stable, as many modern day migrant babies are born in makeshift shelters. Unfortunately, in the United States, detained undocumented mothers who go into labor before being released are hospitalized according to immigration detention policies. They are hospitalized, chained to the delivery bed, and their babies taken away from them at birth. Then the women are returned to detention.

Jesus was one of and one with the marginalized. He was born in poverty, forced to flee to Egypt as a toddler, returned to Nazareth to bring a prophetic word and be persecuted for doing so, and lived an itinerant life reaching out to the least, the last, the lost and the other. Jesus lived a nonviolent life and instructed his followers to do likewise. He taught that the path to eternal life includes loving your neighbor as yourself. In the end, he died a horrendous death because of political and religious accusations. His crucifixion took place on the outskirts of Jerusalem because he was undocumented and did not have the papers of a Roman citizen.

That was not the end. The resurrected Jesus told Mary Magdalene to go and tell the other disciples that he was alive. They then spread the word throughout the world. Mary Magdalene traveled and preached with them. Her mission and ministry is a model for women who have chosen to share the Gospel of Christ throughout the ages.

Following his resurrection, Jesus appeared as the stranger on the road to Emmaus to reconnect with his followers before migrating back to his heavenly home, giving them their great commission to go and tell. This became their mission in the Book of Acts and began a worldwide impetus to spread the good news of the Gospel of Christ.

Jesus also sent the Holy Spirit to be with his followers as a listener, helper, and guide. The Holy Spirit's movement was seen on the day of Pentecost and throughout the New Testament. Key disciples traveled the world spreading the Good news. A circle was completed and the Spirit of God who migrated over the face of the waters continues to migrate today, by accompanying each and every one of us throughout our lives.

As followers of Christ it is important that we realize that Christ is in us and the Holy Spirit is with us. Therefore in everything we do, we are forcing Christ to do with us. The question we must ask is are we asking Christ to participate in thoughts, words, and deeds that reflect a godly view and standard of conduct or that reflect a more worldly view and standard of conduct? How are we responding to the strangers among us? Our response to the stranger is our response to God.

People of all ethnicities, documented and undocumented, add dimensions to the United States that make it a beacon of diversity that has the potential to have ever-changing ramifications for the world. We are a moving kaleidoscope of humanity. Remnants of people from all over the earth reside within our borders. In any kaleidoscope, the image changes continually, but the view is always beautiful and unified through its diversity. Sometimes it is absolutely breathtaking. No single part has the flavor or beauty of the final product. Having been blessed with this diversity we can covenant together in the words of Romans 9:25–26: "Those who were not my people I will call 'my people,' and her who was not beloved I will call 'beloved.' And in the very place where it was said to them, 'You are not my people,' there they shall be called children of the living God."

Historically, many of the citizens of this country came here because they were rejected in their homelands. A new world was created from unwanted and persecuted people. We all must remember that, in the form of our ancestors, we stood on these shores seeking refuge. Each new group was discriminated against and made to feel unwanted. We were once the strangers and must not act in retaliation and hate but rather act in love, kindness, and compassion. Radical, inclusive hospitality seeks actions on religious, social, political, and economic fronts to put an end to racism, prejudice, bias, and exclusivity. As theologians and followers of Christ, we must both interpret and change reality.

Active Theologians

As radical, inclusive, hospitable disciples, we are the world's active theologians. We must revive Christianity so that the diversity of God's people is seen as a unifying factor creating a composite picture of the creator God in whose image we are created. In this way, all people will see themselves and others as created in the image of God and realize that their diversity helps to create the complete image. No one will be troubled or alienated by his or her personal image. Each person's image will be a positive image. Each person will be willing to look in a mirror and unashamedly admit that yes, it is true: he or she was made in God's image and is perfect for the role God has planned for his or her life.

This calls for using the Bible as the ultimate immigration handbook and as a textbook for radical inclusivity by remembering that Christ came in the spirit of freedom, justice, and love. If Christianity is to be the religion of the body of Christ, then it must be a religion that protests exclusivity and injustice. Christ's very life was a nonviolent protest to the injustices of the world. Along with uplifting a variety of images of the Christ, it will also be necessary to change the image of Christianity as we know it.

Perhaps it is time to resurrect the Christ of Martin Luther King Jr., who is, as God is, Love. To begin to visualize Jesus as Love in addition to Jesus as Lord is to begin to chip away at the horrendous structures that perpetrate a classist hierarchy in our world. The Christ of Love and the love of Christ call communities to be involved in social and political issues that will change the fabric of our country. This Christ calls people to protest the social injustices of the world and to work to "let justice roll down like waters, and righteousness like an ever-flowing stream" (Amos 5:24). Is it perhaps time to begin to protest once again? It would seem so, because if the status quo continues, we will all eventually be lost. If we are to change, the change must and will come from within the churches through the word of God lived out in love in the socioeconomic context.

Mr. King wanted the people to work, en masse, to make the laws of equality real and meaningful. He felt that blacks were the instrument that would be used by God to save the soul of the United States. Looking at United State in 2011, especially at the state of interethnic relationships, it appears that the United States' soul continues to be challenged by the forces of evil. Gerald Lenoir, director of the Black Alliance for Just Immigration stated, "Migration is one of the cutting edge issues in the struggle against racism in the United States today. Immigrant rights is an expression of the historical struggle against racism."[3] It is time for all of the people in the pews who know in their heart of hearts that all people are equal to speak out and work together to build radical, inclusive, hospitable communities. Radical, inclusive hospitality is not a planned event or series of gestures or actions. "It is the stance of the heart that is abandoned to love."[4]

It is not too late; there is always a remnant of God's people being called to be the peacemakers in the world. Margaret Mead is credited with saying, "Never doubt that a small group of thoughtful committed citizens can change the world. Indeed it's the only thing that ever has." It is time for us to claim our redemptive role by working to build radical, inclusive hospitable communities.

Mr. King wanted people to accept their redemptive role through embracing five objectives: self-respect, high moral standards, whole-hearted work, leadership, and nonviolence. These five objectives might very well work today in the establishment of a communal church that unites all believers in God's community and uplifts the unifying factors of diversity. This is a concept that can be embraced by each and every church just where it is. There is no cost to do so; it is simply a shift in theology, which requires an effort to be radical, inclusive, and hospitable.

This theology understands Jesus as the loving, liberating God and ancestor of all humankind. This is a theology in which all ancestors—all saints who have gone before—are seen in Christ. Through the realization that we are the ancestors of the future, we can learn to touch our God and ourselves. In this way all will be able to touch our ancestors and our lost identities through Christ and therefore one another.

Community, Diversity, Outreach, and Growth

We will discover that to be fully human and fully alive we must live in community. As creators of radical, inclusive, hospitable communities, we must think "we" instead of "I." We must see Christ in the stranger and realize that the stranger is seeing Christ in us. We are to love God, our neighbors, our selves, and our enemies (real or perceived). In truth, very few people are enemies; however, society has created a "them" and "us" myth.

An important part of living in community is giving up self. This means changing lifestyles and becoming committed to living a simpler life. We must "live more simply so that others may simply live." We must die to self materially, realizing that justice in the Hebrew Bible meant every person would have life's basic necessities. We begin by asking, "Do I have more than I need?" Mercy Amba Oduyoye writes, "Those who believe that Christ lives forever . . . will venture to live a life of total dependence on God by taking what he commands seriously. . . . Whatever the culture, Christ relates to the needs of the people."[5]

We must make justice, mercy, inclusivity, and radical hospitality vocabulary words in all languages. We must insist on living in a community with Christ as the center. We must make it possible for those who have not seen the face of justice to begin to see it repeatedly and for those who do not have the basic necessities of life to be able to live comfortable lives by sharing in God's abundant goodness and goods. As Christians we must base our response to immigrants and refugees on sacred scriptures. There is no scriptural justification for any response to immigrants and refugees other than a response of radical, inclusive hospitality.

Radical discipleship requires Christians to follow the will of God through personal action and example by walking in Christ's footsteps. Hospitality—in its truest form as defined and practiced in the

Hebrew Bible—means welcoming the stranger. Inclusivity means to welcome in and include. Radical means drastically different from the ordinary practice, outside the normal. Planning radical, inclusive hospitality for immigrants and refugees means seeing and understanding their social, political, economic, and religious plights and responding to them.

We live in a culture that has historically shunned persons who are not of white European descent. Racism is pervasive. The United States is called the land of the free, but there are many sins that continue to be perpetrated as the "'isms" continue. We gloss over them and pretend they don't exist. It is impossible to study xenophobia without considering prevailing color and class issues.

It is only necessary to look at the race studies done after Hurricane Katrina to verify that we are a country split over ethnicity and increasingly torn by strife resulting from ethnic and class differences. Almost no media attention was given to the tens of thousands of documented and undocumented migrants who were affected by the hurricane. The situation was largely looked at as a black and white issue, even though the Hispanic population of the United States is larger than the African-American population.

However, the need for the undocumented laborers was recognized when, in the aftermath of Katrina and to stimulate relief efforts, President Bush temporarily suspended portions of the Davis–Bacon Act, which requires construction workers on federal projects be paid the prevailing local wage. In addition, the Department of Homeland Security said it would not penalize employers who hired undocumented workers. The reality is these two actions were giving employers authority to hire undocumented workers for less than the going wage. Actions of this type are not only harmful to the undocumented but also harmful to citizens who will be hired. There is, of course, the possibility that, as in many cases, citizens will be paid at a higher rate than undocumented workers. These actions also demonstrate the fact that no one can take another's job. Employers give jobs to others based on their profit margins. It is also an example of the government not following its own employment rules and regulations.

According to the U.S. Census Bureau 2010 American Community Survey, the ethnic mix in our country is presently 74.0 percent white, 15.7 percent Hispanic or Latino, 12.5 percent black or African American, 4.7 percent Asian, .8 percent Amerindian and Alaska native, and .2 percent native Hawaiian and other Pacific Islander.[6]

Also, the same study indicates undocumented immigrants in the country represented 26 percent of the total foreign-born population. Of the undocumented population, 57 percent came from Mexico, 23 percent are from other Latin American countries, 10 percent from Asia, 5 percent from Europe and Canada, and another 5 percent from the rest of the world.

Since 2007, the number of undocumented immigrants coming into the United States has decreased greatly. The Pew Institute estimates that in 2009 there were 5.8 million undocumented men (a decrease in numbers), 4.2 million undocumented women, and 1.1 million undocumented children. However, 4 million U.S. children have at least one undocumented parent. The number of men, women, and children coming in from Latin American countries other than Mexico decreased by 22 percent. From March 2007 to March 2009, 150,000 undocumented immigrants from Mexico arrived. This was 70 percent below the annual average of 500,000 per year during the first half of the decade.[7] According to the *New York Times*, by July 2011 the "extraordinary Mexican migration" of the past three decades has "sputtered to a trickle." Combining the numbers of undocumented immigrants entering and leaving the country had reduced undocumented immigration to zero.[8]

The faces of immigration differentiate immigration today from immigration of the past. In the early part of the twentieth century, immigrants continued to come to the United States from Europe and were much more easily assimilated into the dominant white Euro-centric culture. Today's immigrants are from other parts of the world, and they are suffering the prejudices and practices of a country that has tolerated and embraced racism for centuries.

The fear of the stranger that is rampant today takes the color factor and compounds it with language and culture factors. Although there are a very large number of documented and undocumented immigrants who come from Europe as well as other areas of the world, the picture painted by the media and the government is one of color and Hispanic ethnicity. In addition, there are movements across the country to make English the official language. One cannot help but wonder if a new twist is being given to the Tower of Babel story. It is also important to remember that, in that story, God rejected the one language concept and sent the builders of the tower throughout the world speaking different languages. God's preference is for multiple languages. Overall, God's preference is for variety, as can be seen by the diversity of the creation and in the diversity of the Trinity.

We have the ability to be linguistically diverse. Very few countries are monolingual. Most nations require at least one other language as part of their educational system. Spanish is gaining in popularity in the United States. There is an urgent need for expanded Spanish as a second language classes, and requests for instruction in Mandarin Chinese are rapidly growing.

Eighty-five percent of immigrants become very adept at speaking English, and many more would if there weren't a severe shortage of English as a second language (ESL) classes. Sometimes immigrants must wait for years to enroll in a language class. In addition, learning a new language can be very difficult, especially for adults. Be patient and understanding with people who speak other languages. Put yourself in their place and try to imagine what you would do if you had to learn a new language, or, even better, do your best to learn at least basic words in another language. Also, offering Spanish as a second language is a way to embrace the stranger and offer additional outreach to your community. Presently, more than 10 percent of our population speaks Spanish. It might be a good place to start learning a new language.

Getting into a language class can be very difficult, and there are simply not enough classes to meet the demand. ESL classes are an excellent way for churches to start community outreach to immigrants. While waiting for ESL classes, most immigrants continue to live within their own culture. This may mean living within a cultural ghetto, which are often systematically planned by the economic advisors of any given city. Just as town rules and regulations continued to separate blacks and whites after civil rights laws were enacted, similar rules and regulations as well as societal practices often segregate immigrants from the majority population. As newcomers, they are forced to live in substandard housing with landlords who pay little or no attention to their requests for repairs. Mainstream society often benefits from these cultural ghettos. Ethnic restaurants and stores abound. The restaurants are embraced and patronized, but their owners and staff are considered to be outsiders and never fully integrated into the community. Restaurants often employ workers at substandard wage while government agencies often ignore practices in restaurants that would result in huge fines and shutdowns in mainstream restaurants. However, immigrants and refugees can provide benefits to dying towns when welcomed.

There is often a double standard, two different sets of responses: enjoying the benefits of other cultures but wanting to deport the providers of those benefits. This is simply another form of prejudice that sees to it that one class of people is kept subservient to another class. Very often capitalistic motivation and preferences can be seen. It is not uncommon for the immigration service to raid farms and companies hiring undocumented workers just before payday or on payday. When raided the day before payday, the company benefits—it never has to pay the wages. When raids are conducted on payday, the immigration branch of the Department of Homeland Security charges the migrants whatever their salary happens to be for transportation back to their home country.

Lewiston, Maine, was dying. According to Jesse Ellison in a 2009 *Newsweek* article, the town center was known as the "Combat Zone." By 2001 young people were continuing to flee the town for better opportunities. There were no jobs, and there seemed to be little hope for the future. Then in 2001 a Somali refugee family was resettled in the area. They were welcomed and treated well, and they began to spread the word that housing was cheap and it "looked like a good place to build new lives and raise children in peace." They spread the word to other Somali refugees who had been settled throughout the United States. This began a secondary migration to Lewiston, "one of the whitest areas of the country . . . with old families that have a reputation for distinct chilliness toward 'outsiders.'" The racial, cultural, and religious differences between the Muslim Somalis and the locals were mind boggling and the town's image so negative it was hard to understand why anyone wanted to move there. The townspeople were afraid of losing the few jobs that remained and having social services overloaded. In 2002 the mayor tried to stop the migration, but the Somalis persisted, and 4,000 new residents moved to Lewiston.

By 2009, instead of 76 ESL students per year, there were 950. New shops, new food, new art, and new culture was everywhere. Karen Jacobsen, director of the Forced Migration Program at Tufts University stated, "Generally, refugees or migrants that come into a town give a new injection of energy. . . and new economic activities." The economic activities are not only on the part of the refugees. Residents have opened new businesses and translation services. The town's business consultant explains that there is a growing understanding and acceptance that immigration is associated with good economic growth.

The cultural diversity has helped the education system. The enrollment at Lewiston campus of the University of Maine has jumped by 16 percent, and Andover College opened a campus in 2004 that had to expand because young people prefer going to a college that has a diverse student population. The Somalis are credited with the growth of the town. Cultural diversity was the missing piece. Mr. Ellison sums up his article with a question: Can the rest of Maine—and other states like it—find their own missing pieces? *From "The Refugees Who Saved Lewiston" by Jesse Ellison*, Newsweek, *January 17, 2009.*

Migrants lose in a number of ways. There are the prevailing opinions that undocumented migrants are draining the public assistance system, taking jobs, and committing a variety of horrendous crimes, which include smuggling drugs and being terrorists. This develops from the tendency to stereotype people of color as unsavory characters. As an example, Middle Easterners are suspected terrorists because of 9/11; however, we do not suspect all white men of being terrorists or potential bombers even though the Federal Building bombers in Oklahoma City were white and U.S. citizens.

Historically, this viewpoint has been held concerning each new group of immigrants coming into the land. As an example, in 1853, the *New York Herald* editorialized, "Had we no Irish, or Germans, or Italians in this country, the duties of a police officer would be sinecure."[9] (They would have been receiving a salary but would have had little or no work to do.) Sadly, these views are often supported by church members, who have forgotten that their ancestors were once persecuted because they were strangers. Many churches work very hard to forget their histories. They have become safe houses for congregants of similar backgrounds. Persons varying from the norm are told in a number of ways that they are not welcome. They don't belong. This ranges from blanket statements that they are in the wrong church to being given a very cold shoulder.

Aiding this attitude is the movement to form congregations that are "ethnically pure." This is reminiscent of the removal of the black worshippers from St. George's Methodist Episcopal Church in Philadelphia in 1787. The impetus for forming these "ethnically pure" churches keeps the white church "pure" as well. When this happens, the full picture of a Christ-centered community of worshippers is not seen, and the rich diversity that can be brought to worship is lost. When this happens, the body of Christ is disabled. To be whole, the body of Christ must be diverse. As stated in first Corinthians 12:17, "If the whole body were an eye, where would the hearing be? If the whole body were hearing, where would the sense of smell be?" The church can be much more vibrant and alive if we see, hear, smell, touch, and taste from the great diversity of God's abundant creation.

The immigrants in the land offer opportunities for developing multicultural churches that become enriched through the development of diversity within church traditions and practices. However, some feel that ethnic churches are better able to serve their congregations and should be developed as such. Of course, this continues the tradition of Sunday mornings being the most segregated time of the week and causes us to question church development. Miriam Adeney addresses this question in her article "Colorful Intiatives."[10] Is cultivating distinct ethnic churches a sin against the unity of the Body of Christ? Must our aim be multicultural churches (and therefore multicultural missions)? "Yes," says Stephen Rhodes in *Where*

The Nations Meet.[11] "No," says Eric Law in *The Wolf Shall Lie Down with the Lamb.*[12] "Yes and No," say Soong Chau Rah in *The New Evangelism*[13] and Edward Gilbreath in *Reconciliation Blues.*[14]

Structures are not the bottom line. All sorts of intra- and interchurch structures can nurture rich cultural identities and deep partnerships. Multiple models are shown in *Missions Have Come Home to America* by Jerry Appleby[15] and *Understanding the Coconut Generation: Ministry to the Americanized Asian Indians* by Sam George.[16] Unity is a powerful theme in scripture (Galatians 3:28; John 17; Ephesians 2; 1 Peter 2:9–10). Equally central is the emphasis on vibrant creativity that gives birth to diversity. Deficient in both, North American churches must cultivate both unity and diversity vigorously.[17]

In looking at church identity we seem to overlook the fact that all churches are ethnic churches of one sort or another. Unfortunately, we don't weigh the ethnicity of members of traditional White churches. However, this does come into play, as does the traditional worship practices of long established churches. A church in South Central Pennsylvania may very well have a German/Pennsylvania Dutch ethnicity that forms their identity. One in Minnesota may worship with a Norwegian flavor. One in Boston might embrace its Irish roots, while a church in Chicago might have an Eastern European flavor. (Church suppers are very often key to the ethnicity of a particular church.) So it is most unfortunate that ethnicity seems to refer to naming groups other than the dominant societal group of a country when in fact we are all the products of ethnic groups that make us who we are. As Christians, our overriding ethnic identity is found in our being created in the image of God and all being a part of the body of Christ to one another and the world.

The people within the church community are afforded opportunities to act in concert as Christ's body by understanding that Christ came not to be served, but to serve. It is the servant model that stands out within this community. All sides of the community work together in a loving, giving, and sharing relationship while practicing radical, inclusive hospitality and incorporating immigrants and refugees into their midst.

Immigrants and refugees, perhaps more than any other groups of people, offer opportunities for unconditional love. Christ did not differentiate according to religion, ethnicity, or class. Often immigrants and migrants arrive with very few belongings. Refugees usually arrive with absolutely nothing. They have only their identity as a human being—a child of God. They come seeking freedom, safety, and the basic necessities of life. They come not understanding the language. Often they come from places that have no electricity or running water or cars or computers or refrigerators or telephones. They think or feel they have nothing to contribute, not even the knowledge of what is the right thing to say or do. They are completely vulnerable, completely dependent. Their very lives depend on the reactions of the Americans who meet and greet them. They are often desperately in need of inclusive hospitality. However, they are a great gift, because by welcoming them, we welcome God and are blessed in the process.

Offering radical hospitality means welcoming immigrants into a space where we are connected and they are welcome. This might be inviting them into our home or church or another institution or group. It can be as simple as baking cookies for the newcomer next door and extending an invitation for coffee or tea or to a social gathering.

Hospitality welcomes the stranger into a safe, personal, and comfortable place, a place of respect, acceptance, and friendship. The stranger is included in a life-giving and life-sustaining network of relationships. Such welcome involves attentive listening, sharing of lives, an openness of heart, a willingness to make one's life visible, and a generosity of time and resources.[18]

Repeatedly, strangers in our land will say the most important thing they received was a phone number from someone who said, "Let's keep in touch," and then took the first steps to make that happen. As disciples of Christ seeking to live lives of service and sacrifice, let us prayerfully consider offering hands of hope that create homes away from home to immigrants seeking new life, new acceptance, and a new place in God's all-inclusive community.

Notes

1. Philip E. Wolgin and Ann Garcia, "What Changes in Mexico Mean for U.S. Immigration Policy," The Center for American Progress, August 8, 2011, www.americanprogress.org/issues/2011/08/mexico_immigration.html.

2. Michael R. Bloomberg, Mayor, City of New York, testimony before the Committee on the Judiciary, United States Senate, June 5, 2006.

3. Carol Barton, "Race and Migration: Ten Years after Durban," September 2011, www.unitedmethodistwomen.org/news/articles/item/index.cfm?id=663.

4. Daniel Homan and Lonni Collins Pratt, *Radical Hospitality: Benedict's Way of Love* (Brewster, MA: Paraclete Press, 2002), 203.

5. Mercy Oduyoye, *Hearing and Knowing: Theological Reflections on Christianity in Africa* (Maryknoll, NY: Orbis Books, 1986).

6. U.S. Census Bureau, "American Fact Finder 2010: Selected Characteristics of the Total and Native Populations in the United States 2006–2010, American Community Survey 5-Year Estimates," http://Factfinder2.Census.Gov/Faces/Tableservices/Jsf/Pages/Productview.Xhtml?Pid=Acs_10_5yr_S0601&Prodtype=Table.

7. Jeffery S. Passel and D'Vera Cohn, "U.S. Unauthorized Immigration Flows are Down Sharply Since Mid-Decade," Pew Research Center, September 1, 2010, http://pewhispanic.org/reports/report.php?ReportID=126.

8. Ibid.; Wolgin and Garcia, "What Changes in Mexico Mean for U.S. Immigration Policy."

9. Ellis Cose, *A Nation of Strangers: Prejudice, Politics, and the Populating of America* (New York: William Morrow and Company, 1992), 138.

10. Miriam Adeney, "Colorful Initiatives: North American Diasporas in Mission," *Missiology: An International Review* XXXIX, no. 1 (January 2011).

11. Stephen Rhodes, *Where Nations Meet: The Church in a Multicultural World* (Nottingham, UK: IVP Books, 1998).

12. Eric H. F. Law, *The Wolf Shall Dwell with the Lamb: A Spirituality for Leadership in a Multicultural Community* (St. Louis, MO: Chalice Press, 1993).

13. Soong Chau Rah, *The New Evangelism: Freeing the Church from Western Cultural Captivity* (Nottingham, UK: IVP Books, 2009).
14. Edward Gilbreath, *Reconciliation Blues: A Black Evangelical's Inside View of White Chrisitianity* (Nottingham, UK: IVP Books, 2006).
15. Jerry Appleby, *Missions Have Come Home to America* (Kansas City, MO: Nazarene, 1986).
16. Sam George, *Understanding the Coconut Generation: Ministry to the Americanized Asian Indians* (Niles, IL: Mall Publishing, 2006).
17. Adeney, "Colorful Initiatives."
18. Christine D. Pohl, *Making Room: Recovering Hospitality as a Christian Tradition* (Grand Rapids, MI: Wm. B. Eerdmans, 1999), 13.

Chapter 3
Migration Then and Now

Go from your country and your kindred
and your father's house to the land
that I will show you.

—Genesis 12:1

Newcomers to a land are part of the ongoing creation process in which God created us to be caretakers, caregivers, and care receivers. There is a dance of creation that causes the kaleidoscope of the universe to constantly move and change. Many church members resist change. They are happy with their church, congregation, and worship service and would like their traditions to stay exactly as they have been for the past oh so many years. This is understandable. Since 1950, for many of us, the world has changed at lightning speed. The church is one place where we can slow down the evolution process. Why does it have to change? Let's keep it just the way it always was. The question is, has anything ever remained exactly the same, and was and is that God's intent? We serve and worship a radically hospitable and creative God who gave us a role in the ongoing creation of God's community. Creation itself continues to evolve. If we are afraid of change, we can look to the beauty of the seasons and realize there is nothing to fear.

Before God brought Adam and Eve into being, a beautiful world had been created with earth, sky, sun, moon, day, night, waters, dry land, deserts, plants, fish, animals, and insects. After all that work God stood in the midst of it all and said, "I'm lonely ... I'll make me a man."* Genesis 1:27 tells us, "So God created humankind in his image, in the image of God he created them; male and female he created them." This is a key passage on how to treat others. If we are created in the image of God, we are all a reflection of God. Therefore we are to give each and every human being the highest respect without regard to who they are or where they come from or what they look like or what documents they do or do not carry.

There are two creation stories in the Bible. The first is the full chapter of Genesis 1–2:3, in which after creating the world and all things in it, God declared that it was very good and rested on the seventh day. In Genesis 2:4–25, God created Adam and then Eve and gave them instructions for living in the garden and dominion over everything. However, they did not follow God's directions and, because of their disobedience, they were exiled (Genesis 3:22–24), but not before God sewed skins together to cover and to protect them. God's concern for people on the move began at this point and continued throughout the Bible, which gives direction for treatment of strangers in any land. Although this text focuses on the treatment of immigrants in the United States, the biblical passages are just as relevant in Mexico, Korea, China, Iraq, or any other nation.

Welcoming the stranger is a central theme of biblical hospitality. It calls for a radical, inclusive hospitality that always makes room for the stranger and excludes no one. The first example of radical hospitality is seen after Cain kills his brother Abel (Genesis 4:8–16). As punishment, God made him a wanderer on the earth. But before sending him away, God put a mark of protection on Cain. The

---

* Lines from the poem "The Creation" by James Weldon Johnson.

criminal migrant was protected so he would not be harmed in his wanderings.[†]

As humans multiplied, the earth's population eventually became corrupt and filled with violence. God's plan included a great flood that wiped out all of humanity except for one small remnant. At over five hundred years of age, Noah was chosen to continue the human race. With the help of his wife, sons, and their wives, he built the ark and filled it with two of each kind of living creature (Genesis 6:5–8:22). Noah's family was forced to flee because of a great flood, which would probably (in today's terminology) be considered the greatest natural disaster in the course of human history, perhaps even greater than the tsunami in 2004, the hurricanes of 2005, and the earthquakes of 2010. These twenty-first century events were of biblical proportions and happened in areas with much denser populations than those of biblical times, so they may have caused more loss of life.

Noah and his family became migrants without a known destination. God blessed the survivors of the flood and told them, "Be fruitful and multiply, and fill the earth" (Genesis 9:1b). Later, scripture tells us that from the three sons of Noah—Shem, Ham, and Japheth—and their wives, the whole earth was populated (Genesis 9:19).[‡]

[†] Today very few migrants are protected. If they are undocumented, they are arrested and placed in deportation proceedings. The exception is asylum seekers, who have been persecuted in their homelands. They are routinely and by law placed in immigration detention and must defend themselves or seek legal assistance from behind bars.

[‡] In today's world, victims of a natural disaster are not considered refugees. Many spend the rest of their lives stranded in a strange country or displaced in their homelands. This includes victims of hurricanes Katrina and Irene, the earthquakes in Haiti and Japan, and the floods in Pakistan. During the first decade of the twenty-first century, Haitians were victims of multiple natural disasters and much social and political unrest. However, although there were repeated calls for Temporary Protected Status (TPS) that would permit Haitians to remain in the United States until country conditions improved, TPS was not granted until 2010.

Haitian Refugees

Haitian asylum seekers have at times succeeded in being granted asylum and given refugee status in the United States.

An immigrant attorney and advocate has worked with many Haitians over the years and shared the following story: A fifteen-year-old Haitian boy witnessed the result of the overthrow of President Aristide. He learned that his brother had been killed because of involvement with the Lavalas, and he was told by friends and family to leave Haiti immediately. He didn't want to believe this but knew it was true and followed adults from his church to the shore where his grandmother put him on a boat to the United States. Even though he did not know how to swim, he was on one of the first boats to leave Haiti.

The teenager ended up living with his aunt in the United States. His attorney told him to come for his asylum hearing dressed for the occasion. She told him to have his aunt get him a suit and to get the pastor to come along for support and that his aunt should also be dressed for court.

The following morning, the attorney was in court with a tough judge and government asylum attorney getting ready for what would be a difficult case. Suddenly, the judge looked in back of the court and started demanding to know who those people were and how they dare come in her court dressed like that. The boy's attorney turned around, and there the boy was dressed for the occasion.

His aunt had gotten him a light blue tuxedo with ruffled shirt and white patent leather shoes. She was a big woman wearing a brightly colored chiffon dress with very large matching hat.

Their pastor was with them in his suit, a tight clergy collar with a very large gold cross on his chest, and carrying a Bible. They were dressed (according to their culture) very respectfully in their Sunday best. The lawyer managed to interrupt the judges' tirade by interjecting, "Judge, he's for real. I told him to dress for court."

The judge looked at her incredulously, then looked at the teen and his aunt even more incredulously. She raised her gavel, brought it down, and said very firmly, "Asylum granted." She then turned to the government attorney and said, "Counsel, you are not going to appeal this case are you?"

The government attorney responded, "No, your honor." The case was over. The Haitian teenager, who had in an instant in Haiti lost his brother, his home, his church, his family, and his culture, was given permission to remain in the United States and rebuild his life. *From personal conversation with attorney involved with this case. Shared with permission.*

Haitians come to the United States seeking new lives. They are often people of great faith and look to churches for radical, inclusive hospitality. One such church is Christ United Methodist Church in San Diego. Pastor Bill Jenkins posted the following on the church's website:

At age forty, while going through some difficult times in my life, I experienced the "open doors, open hearts, and open minds" of a United Methodist congregation. After studying Wesleyan traditions, I realized United Methodists and I shared convictions on such matters as social justice, salvation, human equality, worship, church history, and Christ-like compassion. With United Methodists, I am "at home." I invite you to my spiritual home, Christ United Methodist Church.

Perhaps those words brought Haitians to the church's door.

Christ United Methodist Church in San Diego is a church with HEART, which is the Haitian Emigrants and Refugee Team project. The project had its beginnings in 2009, when a group of Haitians met with Mr. Jenkins seeking a place to worship. The church offered radical, inclusive hospitality and welcomed the Haitians into their congregation. Members of the congregation made it possible for Christ United Methodist Church to provide legal assistance, housing, and religious support for the community. They also became the hub of the Haitian community in San Diego and after the earthquake of 2010, raising over $10,000 for the United Methodist Committee on Relief (UMCOR).

The church's work was recognized widely, and in 2010 the Department of Homeland Security's Immigration and Customs Enforcement (ICE) agency asked them for assistance with Haitian asylum seekers. They were particularly concerned about pregnant women and women with small children who had crossed the Mexican border. The women were in detention and sleeping on concrete floors. The church educational wing was the first home for the women. Later apartments were rented and an office suite transformed into temporary housing for Haitian women and children. Mr. Jenkins said, "Helping these strangers has expanded our family of faith and friends."[1]

Migration Continues

As we continue the biblical migration story, Genesis 10 gives an accounting of the migration of Noah's sons and their descendants as "from these the nations spread abroad on the earth after the flood." Note there was freedom of movement.§

As the family of Noah migrated (Genesis 11), the people of the earth spoke one language. Since they had a common language, they built a tower to the heavens. This did not please God, who "scattered them abroad from there over the face of all the earth. Therefore it was called Babel." The migration story continued with multiple languages developing as the people moved and cultures were created.**

The generations continued on the earth, and the biblical story picked up with Terah (the father of Abram), Abram, his wife Sarai, and Lot, his brother's son, settling in Haran. It is there that God spoke to Abram and said, "Go from your country and your kindred and your father's house to the land that I will show you" (Genesis

---

§ It is theorized that if people were free to migrate anywhere in the world, the world's population would balance out and everyone would be able to meet their physical needs. Much of the world is starving. In 2011, one in six children in the United States was food insecure. The World Hunger Education Service tells us in 2010 there were 925 million hungry people, or one in seven across the world. In East Africa there were eleven million starving people in the largest famine in history. If the products and produce of the world were shared more equitably, the world would be able to sustain all of us. Part of discipleship and radical, inclusive hospitality is being willing to share what we have with those who have not. It is also to recognize that very often men and women cross borders to be able to feed their families (Hunger Notes, "2011 World Hunger and Poverty Statistics: World Hunger Education Service," www.worldhunger.org/articles/Learn/world%20hunger%20facts%202002.htm).

** This also causes one to wonder about the wisdom of those calling for English only in the United States. The first explorers brought Spanish into the New World, which was inhabited by indigenous Native Americans with many languages. Also, the Southwestern states all were originally part of Mexico, so Spanish was their first language. English is the second Western language that was spoken in the United States, and although now the predominant language, it is enhanced by numerous other languages that create our linguistic traditions.

12:1). Abram, Sarai, and Lot became migrants going into and out of Canaan to the hill country east of Bethel. They then journeyed toward the Negreb and because of famine went to Egypt to reside there as strangers (Genesis 12:10). They came out of Egypt and eventually separated, with Lot settling near Sodom on the plain of the Jordan and Abram settling by the oaks of Mamre in Hebron (Genesis 13).[††]

War has a permanent scarring effect. In 2009, two United Methodist pastors, one from Korea and one from the Democratic Republic of Congo, were participating in a hospital chaplaincy residency program. I helped them find a very safe and centrally located apartment directly across from the city's police station. A few days later I visited and discovered two very frightened women. They explained that at around 10 p.m. the previous night they had heard lengthy, horrendous explosions. Every police car left the station, and there was a great deal of noise in the street. They had shut off their lights, closed the blinds, and huddled on the floor until long after the explosions stopped and they felt it might be safe to move around. This is a prime example of local customs and/or traditions terrifying residents new to the United States. The explosions were the fireworks at the end of a winning baseball game. The police cars left to assure that the people leaving the stadium got home without incident, and the noises in the street were those of jubilant, victorious baseball fans! Familiar, friendly sounds can be frightening and fearful to newcomers.

[††] God instructed Abram to migrate just as God continues, to this day, to direct people to migrate and immigrate. Within any faith-based group, many people can be found who have embarked on a faith journey taking them to strange lands because they heard God calling them to migrate or to immigrate for a new job or specific ministry. Presently the United States grants a limited number of religious worker visas each year for denominations to bring church members from abroad to the United States to work in a specific ministry. These workers have the potential to eventually become naturalized citizens.

As disciples, we are to be friends who help newcomers become familiar with their new community. As for me, I'll give a great deal more thought to educating newcomers about local customs.

Forced Migration

In Genesis 14, we see the first of many, many biblical battles. In the war, Lot was taken captive and forced to leave his land. Eventually, Abram rescued him and he was able to return home. It is important to remember that whenever there is a war, there will be refugees and internally displaced persons. War *never* takes place without these populations coming into being as a result of the violence. Although this text will not go into depth in describing the biblical wars, the victims, and the results, the harsh reality is that wherever and whenever war occurs, people are uprooted and families destroyed. Until humankind learns to live in peace, there will be migration stories, refugee stories, and asylum stories. During the Gulf War, Gabriel Habib, then General Secretary of the Middle East Council of Churches was asked, "Both sides say God is on their side. Whose side is God on?" He responded, "God is love. Where there is love there is God. Where there is not love, there is not God." We sometimes force God out of the picture.[‡‡]

[‡‡] In biblical times, as in previous centuries, the majority of victims of wars were the warriors. In the twentieth and twenty-first centuries, the majority of victims are civilians, and the majority of civilians are women and children. Forty-nine percent of the world's refugees are women. Eighty percent of the world's refugees are women and children. Estimates have the women and children killed in conflicts that are presently taking place since 2005 being as high as 90 percent of the victims. They are often referred to as collateral damage. The Iraq war created hundreds of thousands refugees in the Middle East and throughout the world and 2.5 million internally displaced persons within Iraq. See UNHCR Population and Geographical Data Section, Division of Operational Support, "2004 Global Refugee Trends: Overview of Refugee Populations, New Arrivals, Durable Solutions, Asylum-Seekers, Stateless and Other Persons of Concern to UNHCR" (Geneva: UNHCR, June 17, 2005), 5.

Abrahamic Religions

In Genesis 15:13, God told Abram of his role in the migration story. It was stated, "Know this for certain, that your offspring shall be aliens in a land that is not theirs, and shall be slaves there, and they shall be oppressed for four hundred years." God then told Abram that his offspring would come back to the land of Abram in four generations.

The story continued by chronicling Abram and Sarai's desire for children. At Sarai's insistence, Hagar, the Egyptian slavegirl, the foreigner, bore Abram a child, Ishmael. Eventually they were exiled into the wilderness and God promised to make Ishmael a great nation—a similar promise was given later to Isaac (Genesis 21).

Ishmael's modern-day offspring are Muslims, who practice Islam. They populate much of the Middle East, Africa, and Asia, and have spread across the world. Islam is the fastest growing religion in the United States. It is important to look at the geographical location of biblical history and the ethnicity of the patriarchs and matriarchs who are the foundation of the Christian faith. They were Middle Easterners, and their histories can be found in the Koran as well as the Torah and the Bible. Christians, Jews, and Muslims are all the descendants of Abraham, practicing what are called the three Abrahamic faiths.

All three sacred books contain the same migration stories. More than fifty biblical stories are recounted in the Koran and the Torah. These include narratives on Adam and Eve, Cain and Abel, Noah, Abraham, Lot and Sodom and Gomorrah, Joseph, and Moses. Later narratives included in the Koran include the stories of Gideon, Saul, David, and Goliath, the Queen of Sheba, Jonah, and Haman. The Koran also reflects the New Testament narratives of Zechariah, John, Mary (the mother of Jesus), Jesus and others. Mary is the most revered woman in Islamic scriptures, and Jesus is seen as the prophet who came before Mohammed.

The scriptural stories are not identical, as they often have different twists and thoughts; however, they pull all three scriptures together and show that we are all members of the family of Abraham. As members of that family, Christians and Muslims have moved across the world, telling similar stories and being the stranger in many strange lands as we practiced our faiths and welcomed others into our circles. We have developed into the two religions with the most adherents in the world. We can easily say that our migration stories have intertwined, and although we have separated at times, the globalization of the world is bringing us back together again. Perhaps it will be our sacred scriptures and prophets, who were people of peace, that will lead us to a time of world peace.

In addition, Mohammed, like other prophets in the Holy Scriptures, was a migrant and a refugee in exile from Mecca during his life. He was also persecuted for his social and religious beliefs and escaped several assassination attempts. Also, the early Muslim community was almost exterminated in Mecca. Mohammed was a man of peace, who fought a war by leading a coalition of tribes in a campaign of nonviolence. He can be added to the list of world leaders who were prophets of peace and nonviolence, which was a focus of Jesus' life; he practiced nonviolence and in doing so won the victory over Satan, sin, and death.

The Bible tells us "Blessed are the peacemakers," and states, "They shall turn their swords into plowshares." Jesus was a man of peace who refused to sanction any type of violence. In Matthew 26:52, he admonished his disciples, "All who take the sword will perish by the sword." They were not to return violence with violence but to respond to violence with love. His followers were to love their God, their neighbors, themselves, and their enemies. All people, without regard to place of origin, were to be considered their neighbors. They were to live lives filled with good deeds and love. To the early disciple, this meant turning the other cheek, going the extra mile, and caring for the stranger and even the enemy. It also meant being a pacifist.

The Koran is a book of peace, which permits war only in self-defense. In addition, Muslims are to defend the country in which they reside, so if the United States were to be attacked, Muslims would respond in defense of this country. Along these lines, much misinformation has been given concerning jihad. Jihad does not mean only "holy war." It also means "struggle" and refers to the effort needed to practice God's will socially, politically, and personally.

It is estimated that there are 2.1 billion Christians in the world, 1.5 billion Muslims, and 14 million Jews.[2] (Interestingly, it is also estimated that there are 1.1 billion persons who are irreligious, agnostics, or atheists.) As we look at the migration history, we can see Judaism as a foundation for all three religions. However, Jews have sought to maintain a cultural and ethnic identity that is in keeping with the mandates of the Torah, which has kept them by nature an exclusive religion. Historically, Jews have repeatedly been persecuted and exiled from their homeland and areas of residence. They have been immigrants, emigrants, refugees, and asylum seekers. This fact, and particularly the Holocaust, has shaped their identity and religious, political, and social practices. Israel is the homeland for all Jews, and all Jews are welcomed. In 1991, fifteen thousand Ethiopian Jews, who consider themselves the lost tribe of Israel, were resettled from Ethiopia to Israel. In the summer of 2011, in response to the African drought, the final eight thousand Ethiopian Jews were brought to Israel as refugees.

Christians and Jews have been somewhat interdependent over the centuries and maintained good relationships both religiously and politically. Presently, the Jewish population is concentrated in Israel and the United States with over six million of the world's fourteen million Jews residing in each of those countries.

Historically, the Muslims moved in one direction and the Christians in another. In doing so, they spread their religions over much of the world. Islam is seen as a Middle Eastern/Arabic religion and Christianity as a Western religion. However, two major branches of Christianity exist, the Eastern and the Western, and, unfortunately more often than not, the two branches move in completely different circles with major differences in theology and practices. Present worldwide globalization is bringing all of us together, and tensions pit one religious group against the other. Radical hospitality can diffuse this tension.

Religious Persecution

Religious persecution has been rampant throughout the world and history and continues today. The early Christian church suffered repeated persecution during the first three centuries by the Roman authorities. Interestingly, it resulted in the rapid growth of Christianity. The contradiction is that persecution is meant to bring an end to a movement, but often rather than an ending, persecution often increases the strength and numbers of the movement or religion.

In its annual report dated April 29, 2011, the U.S. Commission on International Religious Freedom (USCIRF) listed eight nations marked by the U.S. State Department for "particularly severe" violations of religious freedom. They included Burma, China, Eritrea, Iran, North Korea, Saudi Arabia, Sudan and Uzbekistan. It recommended adding six other countries as religious persecutors: Egypt, Iraq, Nigeria, Pakistan, Turkmenistan, and Vietnam. The religious adherents suffering persecution included Christians, Muslims, Baha'is, and other smaller groups such as Falun Gong.[3]

This USCIRF report gives accounts of torture: "They took me to the station and they tortured me. They used something to tie my thumb and one of my toes and they hung me on the wall for three hours," stated one victim of his persecution. Another stated shortly before his execution, "I believe in Jesus Christ who has given his own life for us. I know the meaning of the cross and I'm following the cross. And I'm ready to die for a cause. I'm living for my community and suffering people, and I will die to defend their rights."

Since September 11, 2001, Muslims in the United States have been targeted, imprisoned, and deported because of their ethnicity and/or religion. Unfortunately, popular and media perception has tended to lump all Middle Easterners together as Muslims and terrorists. This has been most unfortunate, as the word Islam means "submission to the will of God" and is related to the Arabic word "salaam" or peace.

Biblical Hospitality and Refugees

The biblical concept of hospitality is based on offering hospitality to the stranger, the sojourner, the alien, the migrant, and the foreigner. After Ishmael's birth and prior to the birth of Isaac, God renamed Abram and called him Abraham and Sarai became Sarah. At that point we are introduced to the importance of caring for the stranger because we never know when the stranger might be God. In Genesis 18:1–8, God appeared to Abraham as three strangers near the oaks at Mamre. Abraham welcomed them and referred to them as "my Lord" and gave them the best of what he had. This is the first biblical description of radical, inclusive hospitality and giving the very best to strangers—who turned out to be God.

Hospitality to strangers can be verified in Deuteronomy 26, which speaks of being brought into a new land by the Lord. This and many other passages in Deuteronomy, which will be included later, stress the importance of being one with the strangers in the land. Entertaining friends and relatives is a different type of contemporary hospitality. St. Benedict taught, "If we close ourselves to the stranger, we close ourselves to the Sacred. If we lock our doors and bolt our gates, we are forbidding God to come to us."[4] As disciples of the Christ, it is important to ask ourselves how many strangers have felt our hospitality and if the doors to our hearts, homes, and churches are open.

The importance of radical hospitality is seen in the story of Sodom and Gomorrah. Lot welcomed the angels, but the townspeople didn't. Their destruction was a result of their lack of hospitality to the stranger. "Behold, this was the guilt of your sister Sodom: she and her daughters had pride, excess of food, and prosperous ease, but she did not aid the poor and needy" (Ezekiel 16:49). This story not only points to Matthew 10:14–15 and Luke 10:10–12 where Jesus declares certain cities more damnable than Sodom and Gomorrah, because they did not show hospitality and welcome Jesus' disciples. It also shows the importance of listening to God and moving when told to move, without looking back. Lot's wife looked back and became a pillar of salt.

The refugee story is one of not being able to look back, because there is often only death and destruction behind. The refugee seeks refuge and safety and sanctuary. Those of us in safer lands are mandated and blessed to welcome them with open arms. Welcoming refugees, migrants, immigrants, and asylum seekers is an example of radical inclusive hospitality and discipleship. Refugees are concerns of nations across the world, and 147 nations have agreed on refugee protection protocols and signed the United Nations Convention Relating to the Status Refugees of 1951, which was written to protect European World War II refugees, and its 1967 protocol, which removed geographical and time limits. It also defined the rights of asylum seekers and nations granting asylum. It defined a refugee as

> A person who owing to a well-founded fear of being persecuted for reasons of race, religion, nationality, membership of a particular social group or political opinion, is outside the country of his nationality and is unable or,

owing to such fear, is unwilling to avail himself of the protection of that country; or who, not having a nationality and being outside the country of his former habitual residence as a result of such events, is unable or, owing to such fear, is unwilling to return to it.[5]

Methodists have been practicing biblical hospitality to refugees for at least 70 years. The Methodist Committee for Overseas Relief (MCOR) was formed to "respond to the vast needs of human suffering around the world." MCOR was instituted as a temporary relief agency by the Methodist General Conference in 1940, and in 1972 at the General Conference, the United Methodist Committee on Relief (UMCOR) was legislated as a permanent entity under the auspices of the United Methodist Church's General Board of Global Ministries. UMCOR's mission has remained relatively the same since its inception. It is "to provide immediate relief of acute human need and to respond to the suffering of persons in the world caused by natural, ecological, political turmoil, and civil disaster." It is divided into five core service areas: world hunger and poverty, health, refugees and immigration, emergency response, and relief supplies.

UMCOR provides aid to people displaced from their homes due to violence, oppression, and natural disaster. Although it was thought that the flow of refugees would slow after the end of World War II, this has, unfortunately, not been the case. The millions of refugees across the world make this work all the more necessary, and UMCOR depends on the good, kind, and radically inclusive hospitable hearts of United Methodists in the pews to welcome strangers from across the world as part of the resettlement process. Refugee assistance was one of the first and largest areas to which UMCOR provided relief when the committee was first formed. World War II had caused a great influx of refugees fleeing from the war, and the rate never slowed down. Today UMCOR continues to provide refugee aid in crisis areas across the world, working with the Church World Service Immigration and Refugee Program network of a variety of denominations and ecumenical agencies and United Methodist churches. Delays resulting from the introduction of new U.S. Homeland Security checks in February 2011 contributed to a significant drop in U.S. refugee admissions in 2011 (fiscal year October 1, 2010–September 30, 2011), with Church World Service resettling 5,322 (down from 7,055 in 2010) toward a U.S. Refugee Admissions Program total of 56,424 (down from 74,654 in 2010).[6]

This is close to 10 percent of all refugee arrivals in the United States for the year. However, to get a true grasp on the need for resettlement it is important to look at the worldwide figures. The United Nations estimates that 15.4 million people around the world are uprooted from their countries because of persecution and armed conflict.[7] Approximately 805,000 of that number are in need of permanent resettlement to a third country. But throughout the world, only about 80,000—less than one percent of the world's refugees—get the opportunity to be resettled. Many others will spend their lives in refugee camps or as undocumented persons in a country not their own. Across the world thousands of persons have been born and raised in refugee camps with little hope of having a permanent home.[8]

Naomi Madsen, program manager of UMCOR's refugee resettlement ministry, explains that the refugee resettlement is apolitical. It is a ministry that positively impacts both the person involved in the ministry as well as the refugees:

> It is a transformational ministry. The transformation doesn't happen so much to the refugees but rather to people who help them to resettle. It is a miracle when someone is resettled and you get to know a life that you

could not imagine. That offers a chance to realize that someone you thought was completely other is more like you than you ever dreamed possible. Hearing about refugees is not the same thing as becoming a friend and really getting to know them. It is so easy. All you have to do is be a friend to someone, be a neighbor, and change the world. You can change someone else's life, as well as your own, by simply being a friend.[9]

Churches and/or groups of churches working together to resettle refugees and offer radical, inclusive hospitality are always needed. Visit the UMCOR website (www.umcor.org) to learn more about the refugee program. To join United Methodist Women's work for immigrant rights visit www.unitedmethodistwomen.org/act/immigration, and to learn of more ways to support United Methodist Women's international work with refugees, visit www.unitedmethodistwomen.org/give/missionmap.

When resettling refugees, it might initially seem that the present church members are the giving part of the community, but as resettlement and integration progresses and the members of the community begin to know one another, it becomes an educational process. Both sides are enriched through learning about the other's lifestyle, customs, manners, and traditions. The community opens up to the joys of inclusive diversity. It becomes an educational process in which all are both teachers and learners. Very often the receiving community that extended arms of inclusive hospitality reaps much greater blessings than those reaped by the strangers who were welcomed.

It is just as important for the welcoming community to learn about the lifestyle and culture of the persons they are hosting as it is for those persons to learn about life in their new country. Making the effort to learn about the culture of immigrants or refugees shows

In Lancaster, Pennsylvania, a large Nepali family found a new family and grandmother. Their grandmother died in the refugee camp, and 94-year-old Maxine Gould became their matriarch. She is honored at joint family celebrations and holidays. Kate Epperly, whose church resettled the family, says, "This family is family. When things are needed we call one another. It's quite lovely and fills a big family hole in my life. We are kindred spirits who honor the same values and ways of living. It has been a blessing for both families." The Nepali mother has joined the church prayer shawl knitting group. The son is completing his education as a pharmaceutical assistant, and each year when the rhododendrons bloom they all gather as one big family to celebrate and give thanks. *From personal communication with Kate Epperly, Church World Service advisory board member.*

the newcomers that they are truly cared about. It validates their beings, increases self-confidence, and lets them know that they are welcome just as they are.

As physical needs are met, emotional ties develop. Another level of communication develops. Spiritual ties can be very important because, although the differences may be great, there is often a need to turn to the God of the Universe to bring comfort and solace in times of stress. It is important to realize that persons being resettled may not be Christian, but we were all created by the same God, and it is important to respect diverse religious beliefs and customs without attempting to change or convert.

One of my favorite stories shared in Church World Service circles is of a Muslim family resettled in the United States by a United Methodist Church. They really enjoyed the fellowship of the church and so they became Muslim United Methodists. They went to Juma prayers every Friday and church every Sunday. It is possible to be a Muslim/Methodist or Methodist/Muslim. As Jesus said, God's house is a house for people of all nations.

The physical, emotional, and spiritual needs of both the newcomers and the church members are answered through working together to integrate sisters and brothers from other lands into a new culture with Christ as the center and mediator of the relationships.

Immigrants, migrants, and refugees bring with them a wealth of worship experiences and traditions. It is important for the welcoming churches to affirm those traditions and experiences. In addition, it is important that the newcomers be permitted to pray in their first language. The Catholic Church is routinely training priests in Spanish for ministry because in times of stress, it is most important that the people hear scripture in, sing in, and be guided in praying in their first language.

There is resistance to the inclusion of other languages in some churches. The question becomes, "How do very diverse groups of people begin to exist in harmony instead of in dissonance?" Deuteronomy 26 tells us that we are to celebrate with the strangers in our lands. Is it possible that the idea of celebration and rejoicing through music and song might begin a healing of the breaches? "You shall be called the repairer of the breach, the restorer of the streets to live in" (Isaiah 58:12).

Music and Song and Hospitality

Perhaps music and song can break down this resistance. Songs of radical, inclusive hospitality might be what is needed for healing and wholeness to take place between all peoples. This idea can be developed, as protest songs were developed, through songs with lyrics that deliver messages on the Gospel that include Jesus and the development of a new humanity. Songs teach theology and often are the cause of action. Across cultures, Christ stands on the shores of our lives saying, "You, follow me!"

"Heart of America" is a song written by Tim Blixseth in the wake of Hurricane Katrina. Its words help define what we would all like to be. It is a song embracing diversity and offering hospitality: "This is the time, a chance to reach out for your neighbors' hands. We follow different ways and come from different lands."

The song also expresses that we all share the same dream. We must learn to sing and laugh and dance and play together inclusively. We must learn to welcome all our sisters and brothers, without regard to ethnicity, religion, or economic status, and work to create peace together. Perhaps we need to make more use of creative mediums. This is imperative, as hospitality of acceptance will eventually enable us to realize we are all one. All people understand music, and the masses learn theology through song. The divisions among the people of God can be repaired through creatively worded and sung songs that teach radical, inclusive hospitality. "Heart of America" does just that; it was written for the people to be embraced and shared by the people from all the lands that make this the United States. It is time to become united. Hurricane Katrina, the attack on the World Trade Center, and the Federal Building bombing in Oklahoma City have shown us that enemies exist within and without, some look like the majority of U.S. citizens, and others have come from afar, and the greatest disaster can result from the forces of nature.

The disasters have taught us what Christ taught us. There is a great need for love in this world. Through his refusal to respond or retaliate with violence as he walked the road to his crucifixion and by submitting to that crucifixion, Jesus the Christ won the victory over sin and death and evil. Practicing radical hospitality demonstrates love of God, yourself, your neighbor, and your enemy. Throughout history and across the world, as we look at the persons who committed atrocities, we must wonder, would they have acted as they did if they understood love and felt loved? As we ponder and decide to be a part of the refugee resettlement community, keep in mind that refugees have been victims of violence perpetrated by people whose hearts and hands are bent on hitting and hurting. Refugee resettlement offers an opportunity to be the hands of Christ in the world and to reach out to the other with hearts and hands that help and heal. When we reach out our hands, we never know when the hand that reaches back will be that of Christ among us.

Notes

1. From personal communication with Naomi Madsen, United Methodist Committee on Relief, and Christ Ministry Center United Methodist Church's website: www.christsd.com.

2. Adherents.com, "Major Religions of the World Ranked by Number of Adherents," modified August 9, 2007, www.adherents.com/Religions_By_Adherents.html.

3. U.S. Commission on International Religious Freedom, "Annual Report 2011" (Washington, DC: USCIRF), www.uscirf.gov/images/book%20with%20 cover%20for%20web.pdf.

4. Daniel Homan and Lonni Collins Pratt, *Radical Hospitality: Benedict's Way of Love* (Brewster, MA: Paraclete Press, 2002), 203.

5. United Nations High Commissioner on Refugees, "Text of the 1951 Convention Relating to the Status of Refugees," www.unhcr.org/3b66c2aa10.html.

6. Church World Service, "Church World Service Resettles 5,322 Refugees in FY 2011 Toward 56,424 U.S. Refugee Program Total," October 14, 2011, www. churchworldservice.org/site/News2?page=NewsArticle&id=13211.

7. UNHCR, "World Refugee Day: UNHCR Report Finds 80 Percent of World's Refugees in Developing Countries," June 20, 2011, www.unhcr.org/4dfb66ef9. html.

8. UNHCR, "UNHCR Urges More Countries to Establish Refugee Resettlement Programmes," July 5, 2010, www.unhcr.org/4c31cd236.html.

9. Personal communication with Naomi Madsen, UMCOR, 2011.

Chapter 4
Global Migration and Scripture

A wandering Aramean was my ancestor;
he went down into Egypt and lived there as an alien,
few in number, and there he became a great nation,
mighty and populous.

—Deuteronomy 26:5

M igration narratives fill scriptures and have touched each of us theologically, emotionally, and physically. Many of us have some knowledge of our migration narratives, and others of us simply know we are here because of ancestors who migrated to these shores. The global phenomenon of migration is part of the human story. At this time, across the globe there are an estimated 240 million migrants. In recent history, we have seen large populations on the move because they have been forced out of their homelands. Modern-day exoduses continue; however, it must be remembered that there are other large populations who must relocate because of natural disasters. These populations have no legal solution for their situation, and the victims are often internally displaced within their own countries or forced to become undocumented migrants in search of a livelihood.

Modern Exoduses

Tibetans fled their country in 1959 after the takeover by the Chinese, when the fourteenth Dalai Lama fled to India to set up a government in exile with 80,000 people following him. That number has grown with close to 150,000 Tibetans living in exile. Most of them are in India, Nepal, and Bhutan. They continue to be asylum seekers in the United States.

The Cuban exodus also began in 1959 with the Cuban Revolution. Since that time more than one million Cubans have left the Island. Their main destinations have been the United States, Spain, Mexico, Canada, and Sweden. Cubans are welcomed into the United States because they are fleeing a communist government. Cubans who reach the United States and actually land on our shores are almost universally permitted to remain in the country and granted asylum. This is referred to as the wet foot/dry foot policy. Once on land they are deemed to have actually entered the country; if picked up in boats off shore, they have not entered and can be returned.

According to Iraqi Refugee Stories (www.iraqirefugeestories.org), since 2003 two million Iraqis fled the violence of the war in Iraq. Another 2.5 million are displaced within the country. The exodus continues with neighboring countries housing the largest number of Iraqis. Jordan hosts as many as 750,000 refugees, and Syria between 1.5 and 2 million refugees, with several hundred thousand more in Egypt, the Gulf States, Iran, Turkey, and Yemen. By the summer of 2007, 60,000 refugees per month were fleeing Iraq. The number of returnees has been small compared to the refugees who continue to reside in other countries. The United States has resettled 45,000 Iraqi refugees.

Across Darfur in 2011, 2.6 million internally displaced persons lived in large camps. Around 250,000 Darfur refugees live across the Sudanese border in neighboring Chad.[1] Of particular concern has been sexual violence against women and the difficulty humanitarian organizations face that try to assist the survivors of the violence. A turn of events was seen in 2011 with the split of Sudan into North and South Sudan and the creation of a new nation.

Shada fled Iraq with her mother and six siblings after her father was killed at the start of the war. They spent the next four years of their lives in a tent in a refugee camp at the Jordanian border. She sobs as she tells a story of having lost everything and of the fear of living in a tent that sways in the wind when the storms come. After the loss of her father she is most saddened by the loss of years of education. In the camp there were no books, no Internet, no technology, none of the educational benefits she had in Iraq. She says, "We lost our lives. In Iraq I loved Oprah and the American people and their lifestyle. The American people are good, kind people." She feels it is the politicians who have caused the war and the destruction of her life and the lives of so many of her friends. She speaks of lying on her mat and wondering how many of her friends might still be alive and where they are. She fears she will never see them or have a home. (See www.iraqirefugeestories.org for more stories. Shada's story was featured August 18, 2011.)

A historic turn of events took place on July 9, 2011, when South Sudan became an independent nation six years after a peace agreement was made with the government of Sudan. The people of South Sudan are seeking to build a free, democratic, and inclusive society. The formation of the new government involved the United Nations, United States, African Union, European Union, the Arab League, and Sudan's neighbors all supporting the two nations peace agreement and working to help them live in peace with one another.

Another African country, Somalia, has been called the world's worst humanitarian disaster. According to Refugees International, in 2011 there were more than two million Somalis in need of assistance. In addition, 860,000 Somali refugees are officially registered worldwide. Somalia also has more than 1.5 million internally displaced persons (IDPs).[2]

The previous examples concerned refugees who fled because of persecution or fear of persecution because of their race, ethnicity, religion, political opinion, or membership in a particular social group. However, across the globe people are migrating for many reasons. Much of the migration is forced by the poor economic conditions in developing countries.

Indhodeeq Abdulle was a refugee from Somalia in 2006. She was resettled to Columbus, Ohio. Her primary concern was her orphaned grandchildren, who at that time were four, six, and twelve years old. After their mother died, the children had been left with a neighbor in Kenya and were being abused. One was beaten and lost four teeth and another had a head injury as a result of a housekeeper hitting it against a wall.

The U.S. Department of Homeland Security instructed Ms. Abdulle to "file" for the grandchildren. However, there is no legal channel through which she could file for them. Her only hope was a Priority-1 (P-1) referral reserved for persons with compelling protection needs.

Angela Plummer, who directs Community Refugee and Immigration Services (CRIS) for Church World Service's Columbus, Ohio, affiliate, referred the case to Mapendo International, whose mission is to protect at-risk and forgotten refugees in Africa. A P-1 approval was given, and on February 25, 2009, Ms. Abdulle's grandchildren, Samira, Khalid and Sulekha, arrived in Columbus—straight into Ms. Abdulle's arms.

At that point, the community became involved and as part of their "Make a Difference" unit at school, Ms. Plummer's son's first grade class at Wellington School collected books, backpacks, school supplies, clothes, shoes, toys, blankets, towels and sheets for the grandmother and her grandchildren. Ms. Abdulle is now a different person! Her grandchildren are enrolled in school, and she is appreciative to be with them and for their new life. For the CRIS staff, it is a blessing to be part of their story and their lives. *From "Three Somali Orphans Reunited with Their Grandmother" by Angela Plummer in* Welcome *4, no. 4 (June–July 2009),* www. churchworldservice.org/site/DocServer/index.pdf?docID=1681.

Border Crossers

People are on the move more now than ever before. (For an interactive overview of the world's population according to country, visit the Migration Policy Institute's Interactive Data Hub at www.migrationinformation.org/datahub/wmm.cfm.) Europe and the United States receive the most migrants. Ireland, Italy, Greece, and Spain, whose citizens historically migrated, many to the United States, are now receiving the largest numbers of migrants. Large numbers of Africans are migrating to European countries, as are migrants from Eastern Europe. The United States receives the largest number of migrants from the global south, with Central Americans making up more than half of the undocumented migrants in the country.

Migration is driven by political and economic necessity. According to Bread for the World, close to half of all Mexicans live in poverty. Eighteen percent live in extreme poverty and can't meet their food needs. Fifty percent of Guatemalan children are malnourished, and almost half of the people in Nicaragua live on less than one dollar per day. Unless poverty is addressed and economic development increased, northern migration will continue.[3]

A few years ago, I was blessed with meeting José (not his real name) and his family. I was with a group investigating causes of Mexican migration. He greeted us by offering bottles of Coca-Cola to thank us for his having been able to cross the border to work for fifteen years during the harvest season to feed his family. He had crossed each year with the same coyote (smuggler) but feared that the militarization of the border would halt his migration and make it impossible for him to continue to support his family.

Marta (not her real name), his twenty-year-old daughter, was working in a sewing factory in Mexico. The long hours and abusive conditions were taking a toll on her. However, she feared crossing the border, as the Mexican states had been instructed by U.S. officials to crack down on persons crossing state borders to head north. Young women wishing to cross borders were routinely required to have sex with border officers to get through. She was a young woman of deep faith and feared taking the risk of crossing the border. However, if she could find no other way for her family to eat, she admitted she would probably attempt the journey north and pray for a safe passage and work on the other side.

It was frightening to look in the face of a young woman who was working ten or twelve hours per day in a factory owned by someone in the United States and making only seventy dollars per week. From this money she was required to pay for her transportation and lunch every day. She was also required to take a birth control pill on the way into work each day. All female employees of the factory had to do so to ensure they did not get pregnant by a boyfriend, husband, or any of the plant managers who would use them for their pleasure. If they did become pregnant, they would eventually have to take time off from work, and that was not permitted.

It was humbling for our group to drink the soda offered. We knew José could not afford to give more than a dozen of us soda, but it was his joy and his thanks because we represented the United States. His family showed radical hospitality by welcoming us and offering their form of a cup of cold water. As we accepted the gift of friendship, it was impossible not to think of the border's dangers. Women crossing the border are vulnerable targets for sexual assault. A United Nations representative estimated that 70 percent of unaccompanied women who cross are sexually assaulted. In addition, they are advised to take birth control pills in anticipation of the assaults.[1]

In the summer of 2011, it was very difficult to cross the Mexican border. Not only were there border guards to deal with, the increasing drug cartels had moved in and were terrifying migrants as they sought control of travel routes through Guatemala and Mexico into the United States. Migrants had additional dangers of being robbed or forcibly recruited into the cartels' service. On August 30, 2010, BBC reported the death of the mayor of a Mexican border town and the investigation of a mass murder of 72 migrants believed to be the work of a drug cartel.[5] Since that time the deaths have increased. The danger for migrants has increased. Those who continue to cross do so often stating they trust that God will be with them.

Moses's Story

People are uprooted for multiple reasons, and only a few have been mentioned. The Book of Exodus records of one of the earliest records of a people being uprooted. It is the story of the movement of the people of God away from slavery and injustice to freedom and new life. It is perhaps the world's greatest and best-known migration story. Exodus began with the Hebrews—who generations earlier had migrated to Egypt in the face of famine—being enslaved by their taskmasters. Their persecution was increased with the orders of the King of Egypt to have all newborn Hebrew boys killed. However, one child was protected and hidden until he was three months old, at which time he was placed in a basket in the river. In today's language he would be referred to as an "unaccompanied alien child." The child was rescued from the river by Pharaoh's daughter, who chose to ignore her father's orders to kill all male infants. She named him Moses, and raised him in Pharaoh's palace.*

Moses grew up to witness the oppressive treatment of the Hebrews by the Egyptians. In responding to this injustice, he killed an Egyptian and became a criminal alien who fled for his life to a strange land. He was taken in and given sanctuary in Midian.†

In Midian, Moses married Zipporah and was called by God to return to Egypt because, in God's words, "The cry of the Israelites has now come to me; I have also seen how the Egyptians oppress them. So come, I will send you to bring my people, the Israelites,

---

* Unaccompanied children picked up at a U.S. border, unless immediately returned to their country of origin, are placed in juvenile detention facilities until they can be placed in foster care. According to Kids in Need of Defense (see www.supportkind. org), in 2010 more than eight thousand minors arrived in the United States without parents or guardians. If detained they are placed in foster care until a decision about their immigration status is reached. Many others live in the shadows in fear of being picked up by the authorities and returned to their home countries.

† Today in the United States Moses would be put in prison to serve his sentence. On completion of that sentence he would immediately be moved to an immigration detention center. He would eventually be deported to Egypt, to be imprisoned there if the country would accept him.

An infant under two years of age was held in a facility in Texas that is one of three sites for unaccompanied infants who are waiting for family reunification or foster care in the United States. The child had been on a bus with parents in Mexico heading for the border. The bus was stopped by banditos. When the child's parents were grabbed, the mother handed the baby to a stranger, another woman, and pleaded, "Please—please, take care of my child and get her to safety." The mother and others were taken outside and executed.

The bus crossed the border and was stopped by the U.S. Department of Homeland Security's Immigration and Custom Enforcement officers. The woman told them the baby was not her child, that the child's mother had been shot and killed. Officials on the Mexican side of the border located the grandparents, who at first said they would take the child. However, the grandparents later denied the child. It is believed they feared for their safety. The child was returned to a sixty-four bed shelter to wait for a resolution to her case. *From personal communication with an attorney who wishes to remain anonymous.*

out of Egypt." Moses wondered how he could possibly do this, and God replied, "I will be with you" (Exodus 3:1–12). The key phrase was "I will be with you," and God was with the Hebrews in the Exodus.

Moses returned to Egypt and led the Exodus after a series of plagues and dialogues with Pharaoh brought about the release of the Hebrew people. When the Hebrew people were finally permitted to leave, they left as most refugees leave, with not enough time to pack, but with God leading them. As with all refugees, the Hebrews had to leave abruptly and leave forever, heading to an unknown but promised land.[‡]

In analyzing the situation in Egypt, we see parallels to the contemporary migration story. We can go back to the time of Joseph who was able to rise to prominence in Egypt. When his family was forced to flee because of famine, he gave them shelter in Egypt. They multiplied, and the Hebrews became an integral part of Egypt's economy and labor force. At first they were welcomed, and then as they grew in number were looked at with suspicion. They didn't fit into the culture, had a different religion, looked different, were not citizens, and were threatening the national image. Pharaoh tried to eliminate the male children. To control them, restrictions were placed on them. They were forced to work in horrible conditions for low wages to increase the profit margins for the people in power. The Egyptians had forgotten the migrants' contributions, and they were no longer welcome. Pharaoh was afraid the face of the nation would change and the Hebrews would outnumber the Egyptians, so he hardened his heart and enslaved them. However, in response to Moses, Pharaoh eventually gave permission for them to leave on short notice. Once they left, Pharaoh realized the disastrous ramifications of losing a major part of Egypt's workers. He also realized what removing so great a number of people would do to the economy. Pharaoh realized the mistake he had made and sent his army after them saying, "What have we done, letting Israel leave our service?" (Exodus 14:5). Economic disaster was pending.

[‡] Ask yourself, what would you bring if you had less than fifteen minutes to pack to leave your home forever? This is a decision that modern-day refugees are repeatedly forced to make. The Hebrews left, but their actual status could be debated. They were forced to work in impossible conditions, their pay was not a living wage, and they had harsh task masters; however, if their treatment did not rise to the level of persecution, they would not be considered refugees but rather migrants looking for work.

In Exodus 13:17–22, we read,

> When Pharaoh let the people go, God did not lead them by way of the land of the Philistines . . . God led the people by the roundabout way of the wilderness toward the Red Sea. . . . The Lord went in front of them in a pillar of cloud by day, to lead them along the way, and a pillar of fire by night, to give them light, that they might travel by day and night. Neither the pillar of cloud by day nor the pillar of fire by night left its place in front of the people.

Notice the important line "God led the people." God migrated with the people. God was, is, and always will be with the migrating, uprooted people of the world, seeking to protect them and find safe haven for them. It is also important to remember that this migration pattern included care of the migrants. God provided manna and water and all they needed to survive.[§]

There are far too many deaths in the Southwest desert in the United States. The Rev. Barb Dinnen of Las Americas Faith Community of Trinity United Methodist Church in De Moines, Iowa, is all too familiar with the scenario. She writes of the death of a member of her congregation who had been deported and sought to return to be with family:

> Maria died at 7 p.m. on Monday night, but the coroner didn't register her death officially until Tuesday morning.

[§] In the Southwest, ministries such as Humane Borders and No More Deaths help migrants crossing the treacherous desert areas by putting water stations in frequently traveled areas and going into the desert to look for migrants in distress. Just as God provided water to the Hebrews wandering in the desert, members of this group provide water to the thirsty and medical help to the dying in the deserts of the U.S. Southwest.

He said the official cause of death was exposure, meaning exposure to the heat and cold, sun and drought of the desert that she crossed from Mexico to Arizona. I guess I would say she died of exposure not only to the cruel elements of nature but to cruel, unjust immigration laws, to cold hearts and hot tempers driven by fear of the privileged population believing the "Marias" of the world want to "take from" them. Her body would have been left along the way, unidentifiable, unburied, abandoned to the forces of nature were it not for another migrant who, once she died, carried her through the night. In handing over her body for burial, he knew he was in fact handing himself over for deportation, but as he had said to the coyote, "She is a human being, not an animal. I am not leaving her here!" (The complete story can be found in the appendix of the participant's guide. From personal communication with Barb Dinnen.)

Eventually the Hebrews reached Canaan and prepared to take over the Promised Land. They entered and took the Canaanites' land away from them, and the Canaanites became refugees and internally displaced persons. They were made to do forced labor for the conquering Hebrews. The joy of the Hebrews resulted from the destruction and displacement of the Canaanites. There cannot be victors without victims.[**]

Along with the details of entering the Promised Land, the Bible also contains advice on how people are to act once they are in a land and others enter. One of the first instructions is found in

---

[**] Details can be found in Exodus, Numbers, and Deuteronomy. An example that is even closer to home is the knowledge that the indigenous people of North America, the Native Americans, were decimated from disease and violence and placed on reservations. Their homeland was taken away from them so others could claim it as their promised land.

Deuteronomy 10:17–19:

> For the Lord your God is God of gods and Lord of lords,
> the great God, mighty and awesome, who is not partial
> and takes no bribe, who executes justice for the orphan
> and the widow, and who loves the strangers, providing
> them food and clothing. You shall also love the stranger,
> for you were strangers in the land of Egypt.

There is a great need for churches willing to develop programs of radical, inclusive hospitality to strangers. For some reason, the biblical mandate to care for the stranger has not been widely embraced. Very often churches that do outreach to the stranger find they are greatly blessed.

Deuteronomy has long been a basis for ministries to the uprooted. It includes numerous statements on how God's people are to care for the stranger in the land. In Deuteronomy 14:29 we read,

> The Levites, because they have no allotment or inheritance with you, as well as the resident aliens, the orphans, and the widows in your towns, may come and eat their fill so that the Lord your God may bless you in all the work that you undertake.††

Additional passages on the subject in Deuteronomy are the following:

- Deuteronomy 23:7: You shall not abhor any of the Edomites, for they are your kin. You shall not abhor any of the Egyptians, because you were an alien residing in their land.

---

†† Our blessings from God are directly dependent on our welcoming the stranger. God blesses us with grace and expects us to respond to our blessings by blessing others.

- Deuteronomy 24:17: You shall not deprive a resident alien or an orphan of justice; you shall not take a widow's garment in pledge.
- Deuteronomy 24:19–22: When you reap your harvest in your field and forget a sheaf in the field, you shall not go back to get it; it shall be for the alien, the orphan, and the widow, so that the Lord your God may bless you in all your undertakings. When you beat your olive trees, do not strip what is left; it shall be for the alien, the orphan, and the widow. When you gather the grapes of your vineyard, do not glean what is left; it shall be for the alien, the orphan, and the widow. Remember that you were a slave in the land of Egypt; therefore I am commanding you to do this.

All of Deuteronomy 26 is important, as it shows the relationship between each and every person's ancestry and the responsibility that is placed on the people of God to care for the alien. One example is Deuteronomy 26:5b, which reads, "A wandering Aramean was my ancestor; he went down into Egypt and lived there as an alien." We are reminded that we all spring from wanderers on the earth. Each of us can state, "A wandering _____ was my ancestor." We all have one or more nationalities or ethnicities to put in that blank space. And we all go back to Adam and Eve.

Deuteronomy 26:10 continues that you shall set down the first of the fruit of the ground and bow before the Lord. "Then you, together with the Levites and the aliens who reside among you, shall celebrate with all the bounty that the Lord your God has given to you and your house" (26:11). The chapter then expresses the importance of caring for others, and in 26:12, during the third year, which is the year of the tithe, the tithe is to be given "to the Levites, the aliens, the orphans, and the widows." The sacred portion is given to these groups at God's command. Once again, God's mandate is affirmed, and it foreshadows the New Testament mandate to care for those in need.

In fact, care of the alien is so important that Deuteronomy 27:19 declares, "'Cursed be anyone who deprives the alien, the orphan, and the widow of justice.' And all the people shall say, 'Amen!'"‡‡

The Psalms and the Uprooted

Along with Genesis, Exodus, Leviticus, and Deuteronomy giving guidance for treating refugees, we also find advice in Psalms. It is important to note that refugees will often refer to the Psalms that they had read and recited to themselves as they were fleeing and seeking a safe haven. One that is used very often is Psalm 91, which begins:

> You who live in the shelter of the Most High, who abide in the shadow of the Almighty, will say to the Lord, "My refuge and my fortress; my God, in whom I trust." For God will deliver you from the snare of the fowler and from the deadly pestilence; he will cover you with his pinions, and under his wings you will find refuge.

As well as giving hope to the uprooted people of the world since biblical times, the Psalms also define the refugee experience. This is best seen in Psalm 137:

> By the rivers of Babylon—there we sat down and we wept when we remembered Zion. On the willows there we hung up our harps. For there our captors asked us

---

‡‡ There is a translation that reads, "Cursed is the nation." Perhaps this is a prophetic warning for governments to consider closely as they seek to close borders, detain immigrants, separate families, and increase deportations.

for songs, and our tormentors asked for mirth, saying, "Sing us one of the songs of Zion!" How could we sing the Lord's song in a foreign land?

This remains the question for all persons who are uprooted in this century. How can they sing in a foreign land, especially one that does not welcome them and in fact seeks to expel them and treat them as less than second-class citizens? A contemporary version of this psalm, as it applies to migrants crossing the U.S. southern border, follows:

> By the waters of the Rio Grande, there we sat down and there we wept when we remembered Zion. On the willows there we hung up our guitars, for there the border patrol asked us for songs and the vigilantes asked for laughter, saying, "Sing us one of the songs of Zion!" How could we sing the Lord's song in a foreign land? By the waters we weep and we remember. We remember Mexico and El Salvador. We remember Honduras and Darfur. We remember Colombia and Bosnia. We remember Cuba and Haiti. We remember China and Romania. By the waters we remember. On the willows we hung up our guitars. We hung up our hopes. We hung up our homes, our land, our dreams. We hung up our poverty, our hunger, our thirst. We hung up our friends, our traditions our culture. We hung up our family ties, our food, our language. How shall we sing the Lord's song in a foreign land? We sing only the song of the homeless, the unemployed, the laments of hunger and thirst, of death and destruction, the songs of the songless, the hungry, the thirsty, the songs of the lonely, the songs of the dying. How shall we sing the Lord's song in a foreign land?

The Prophets

This question was asked by almost all of the prophets, as they were sent to strange lands to follow God's voice. Elijah the Tishbite, after predicting a great drought (1 Kings 17:1–6) was told to flee and hide in the Wadi Cherith where he would be fed bread and meat by the ravens and have water to drink from the brook. As his prediction was correct, the brook eventually dried up and the Lord sent him onward to Zarephath of Sidon to stay in the home of a widow who had been commanded to supply him with food.

Interestingly, Sidon was not part of the kingdom of Israel. The people who lived there were Gentiles. Elijah was sent as a stranger to strangers to seek safety and sanctuary with a widow who was among the poorest of the poor. Although not a Jew, the Gentile widow heard the voice of God. Often the poor are the first to extend radical, inclusive hospitality.

In the Hebrew Bible, just as in the New Testament, we learn repeatedly that God speaks to, answers prayers of, and uses people of all faiths to bring about God's will. The widow followed God's instructions and discovered that the little flour and oil she had multiplied and would not be used up until it rained once again. She also received an additional benefit for helping a stranger when her son died and Elijah cried out to God and restored the child's life.

This biblical passage can be enhanced by reading Psalm 146, which is a Psalm of hope centered in God and mentions the plight of the widow and the orphan at the end. It is a Psalm that uprooted persons can cling to, especially the large percentage of persons on the move who are widows and orphans, oppressed, and hungry. It also speaks to those of us who are concerned about world migration, as it shows the path we are to take as the living hands and feet of Christ.

Praise the Lord! Praise the Lord, O my soul! I will praise the Lord as long as I live; I will sing praises to my God all my life long. Do not put your trust in princes, in mortals, in whom there is no help. When their breath departs, they return to the earth; on that very day their plans perish. Happy are those whose help is the God of Jacob, whose hope is in the Lord their God, who made heaven and earth, the sea, and all that is in them; who keeps faith forever; who executes justice for the oppressed; who gives food to the hungry. The Lord sets the prisoners free; the Lord opens the eyes of the blind. The Lord lifts up those who are bowed down; the Lord loves the righteous. The Lord watches over the strangers; he upholds the orphan and the widow, but the way of the wicked he brings to ruin. The Lord will reign forever, your God, O Zion, for all generations. Praise the Lord!

The story of uprooted people and prophets continued throughout the Hebrew Bible as the Hebrews claimed the Promised Land and were eventually sent into exile and later repatriated. This pattern can be followed in Kings, Chronicles, Esther, Jeremiah, Isaiah, Ezekiel, and Amos.

In 605 BCE, Daniel and his three friends were captured by Nebuchadnezzar and taken to Babylon and renamed Belteshazzar, Shadrach, Meshach, and Abednego. Their God accompanied them even to the point of walking with and then rescuing them from the fiery furnace. Eventually the prophets Ezekiel and Isaiah were also in exile. It is while in exile that Isaiah prophesies the coming of the Christ. See Isaiah 40–55. The time of exile was a time of prophecy preparing the way of the Lord. In Isaiah 40:3 we read, "A voice cries out: 'In the wilderness prepare the way of the Lord, make straight in the desert a highway for our God.'"

In Isaiah 61:1–2a we read the words that are on the scroll that Jesus reads when he first stands up to read in the synagogue to formally begin his ministry. They are: "The Spirit of the Lord God is upon me, because the Lord has anointed me; he has sent me to bring good news to the oppressed, to bind up the brokenhearted, to proclaim liberty to the captives, and release to the prisoners; to proclaim the year of the Lord's favor."

To get the full impact of this passage, it is important to study Luke 4:14–30. It is a key to Jesus' ministry and our care of humankind without regard to their national origins or status. Jesus ends the passage from Isaiah at a crucial point. He stops before saying, "and the day of vengeance of our God." He eliminates the concept of the vengeful, warrior messiah that was to come and vindicate the Jews. He reminds them that a prophet is not accepted in his hometown. And after saying, "But the truth is," Jesus goes on to explain that Elijah was sent to a widow in Sidon and Elisha cleansed a Syrian, a foreigner who came to him, neither of them Jews. Jesus sounded his call for peace by saying that all persons could be recipients of God's love, grace, and miracles. Jesus and the prophets crossed religious borders by ministering to the other. He outraged everyone in the synagogue, and they drove him out of town to throw him off a cliff. "But he passed through the midst of them and went on his way." Jesus and the prophets had no ethnic or religious boundaries.

The prophet Amos called for justice to roll down like water and righteousness like an ever-flowing stream (Amos 5:24). In God's economy, all people are sisters and brothers and share equally and are welcomed. The stranger is cherished and welcomed.

In the Hebrew Bible, everyone was on the move, and most went into exile. This included the prophets, the priests, and the people. Exile shows no mercy. However, some did not go into exile. 2 Kings 24:14 explains, "He carried away all Jerusalem, all the officials, all the warriors, ten thousand captives, all the artisans and the smiths; no one remained, except the poorest people of the land."

This situation continues today. It is not uncommon for the poorest to be left behind. They are not able to pick up and move and must remain in horrific conditions. Some are internally displaced and move within the country seeking safety and care of their basic needs. Others are referred to as the internally stuck, for whom fleeing is not a possibility. This situation struck home in the United States in 2005 when the poorest of the poor were unable to flee the Gulf Coast during and after Hurricane Katrina. It has been repeated in Iraq, Afghanistan, and throughout the world. The horrendous earthquakes in Haiti and Japan and floods in Pakistan have seen the same results. Very often the poorest of the poor remain behind to die or to rebuild their homes and country.

In 2010 the United Nations High Commission for Refugees (UNHCR), stated that there were 27.5 million persons internally displaced because of conflicts with millions more displaced because of natural disasters.[6]

Whether they are left behind, forced to flee, leave by choice, or because they have no other choice, migrants of all faiths turn to scripture to give them strength and courage on their most difficult journeys. Psalm 91 speaks to the plight of the uprooted.

> You who live in the shelter of the Most High, who abide in the shadow of the Almighty, will say to the Lord, "My refuge and my fortress; my God, in whom I trust." For he will deliver you from the snare of the fowler and from the deadly pestilence; he will cover you with his pinions, and under his wings you will find refuge; his faithfulness is a shield and buckler. You will not fear the terror of the night, or the arrow that flies by day, or the pestilence that stalks in darkness, or the destruction that wastes at

noonday. A thousand may fall at your side, ten thousand at your right hand, but it will not come near you. You will only look with your eyes and see the punishment of the wicked. Because you have made the Lord your refuge, the Most High your dwelling place, no evil shall befall you, no scourge come near your tent. For he will command his angels concerning you to guard you in all your ways. On their hands they will bear you up, so that you will not dash your foot against a stone. You will tread on the lion and the adder, the young lion and the serpent you will trample under foot. Those who love me, I will deliver; I will protect those who know my name. When they call to me, I will answer them; I will be with them in trouble, I will rescue them and honor them. With long life I will satisfy them, and show them my salvation.

In Psalm 91, God's promise to give refuge is vividly heard. Throughout the Bible, God admonishes us to care for the stranger; often those who do so are suffering as well. Job knew the importance of caring for the stranger. In Job 31:32, he states, "The stranger has not lodged in the street; I have opened my doors to the traveler." Job was a righteous man who cared for the stranger. How many of us can say that? At this time, we have the opportunity to do just that. The present fear of the stranger in the United States and the targeting of undocumented workers, immigrants, and asylum seekers of certain ethnicities are providing an opportunity for churches to renew and reinstate the biblical concept of radical, inclusive hospitality that is mandated in both the Hebrew Bible and the New Testament.

The Hebrew Bible closes with an admonition from God through the prophet Malachi, who, in Malachi 3:5, repeats the words of the Lord of Hosts,

Then I will draw near to you for judgment; I will be swift to bear witness against the sorcerers, against the adulterers, against those who swear falsely, against those who oppress the hired workers in their wages, the widow and the orphan, against those who thrust aside the alien, and do not fear me, says the Lord of hosts.

This is a very strong statement against exploitation of undocumented workers and day laborers and against people and governments who mistreat the strangers in their land. It is an appropriate precursor to the New Testament and the ministry of Jesus. The Hebrew Bible describes God's love of and care for the strangers. It also demonstrates that God travels with each and every migrant and repeatedly details the importance of our caring for the stranger as we live out lives of service and sacrifice. As twenty-first century Christians it may be helpful as we contemplate ministries of radical, inclusive hospitality to remember that our thoughts become our words, our words become our actions, and our actions become our destinies.

Notes

1. Refugees International, "Sudan," www.refintl.org/where-we-work/africa/sudan.
2. Refugees International, "Somalia," www.refintl.org/where-we-work/africa/somalia.
3. Bread for the World Institute, "Institute Notes: Unauthorized Immigration, Hunger, and Poverty," September 2010, www.bread.org/institute/research/factsheets/unauthorized-immigration_hunger-and-povety.pdf.
4. Tim Vanderpool, "Price of Admission," *Tucson Weekly*, June 5, 2008. See also Human Rights Watch, *Detained and Dismissed: Women's Struggles to Obtain Health Care in United States Immigration Detention* (New York: Human Rights Watch, 2009), 54.
5. "Mexico Mayor Killed as Tamaulipas Violence Escalates," BBC News, August 30, 2010, www.bbc.co.uk/news/world-latin-america-11127005.
6. United Nations High Commission on Refugees, "Working with the Internally Displaced," www.unhcr.org/4ec230ebb.pdf.

Chapter 5
Families, Trafficking, and Slavery

Do not press me to leave you or to turn
back from following you! Where you go,
I will go; where you lodge, I will lodge;
your people shall be my people and
your God my God!

—Ruth 1:16

T he migration story is central to understanding our biblical ancestry and faith perspective on offering radical hospitality. God's people have been on the move throughout history. Women and children have routinely been impacted more adversely by the causes of migration. In the twenty-first century, women make up at least half of the migrating population, and the percentage of women migrants increases each year.[1] Immigrants include everyone from the workers looking for a job and a better life to the Americans who migrate to warmer climates in countries that offer them a higher standard of living on their Social Security and retirement income. It is believed that there are more than two hundred million migrants living outside their home country for at least a year.

Family Reunification

Family reunification is one of the most common causes of migration. Not a simple process, it can take many years for family members to be reunited and at times takes most unfortunate twists. During this time, families are torn apart and miss supporting one another through many of life's milestones, trials, tribulations, and joys.

There are two categories of family reunification: (1) immediate relatives of U.S. citizens (including nonnative spouses of U.S. citizens), unmarried minor children (age twenty-one or younger), orphans adopted by citizens, and parents of adult U.S. citizens, and (2) family sponsorship according to preference categories: unmarried adult (age twenty-one or older) sons and daughters, married sons and daughters, brothers and sisters of adult U.S. citizens, and spouses and unmarried sons and daughters of U.S. permanent resident aliens.*

Many migrants leave their loved ones to seek employment and send money (known as remittances) home. Some of us wonder how anyone can leave his or her children and migrate to another land for work. It seems almost unthinkable, but if we were living in poverty in an undeveloped country and making one dollar a day (or less), we would begin to understand the drive to migrate to the nearest developed country. The options are to migrate or watch children and loved ones starve. According to the World Bank, in 2011 there were more than 215 million migrants across the globe, or 3 percent of the world's population. They sent about $351 billion dollars back to their home countries.[2]

In very poor countries it is not uncommon for a mother to have to decide which child she feeds and which child she lets starve. During

---

* The family reunification process is very complicated. For further information on this topic please visit U.S. Citizen and Immigration Services website at www.uscis. gov, particularly the "Family" section of the site, which provides full information on the rules and regulations of family reunification.

2011 as famine spread over the Horn of Africa, we watched story after story of families walking for days to a refugee camp seeking medical aid and food. National news showed a mother with a two-year-old child weighing seven pounds and others carrying emaciated children dying in their arms. Stories were told of leaving children and family members to die under trees as the family moved on to seek help for the living. They walked for food, for life, for work and in hope of finding radical, inclusive hospitality and people who would recognize their humanity and give them a chance at new life.

Although there is a tendency to think that everyone wants to come to the United States, the world's immigration population is widely distributed. According to the United Nations, in 2007 there were more than seventy countries with immigrant populations of at least 10 percent.[3] The United States does have the largest number of foreign-born residents but a much smaller percentage of foreign-born than many other countries. Globally, the percentages are much higher. In the Persian Gulf, 80 percent of Qatar's population consists of foreign guest workers. Also, if we compare undocumented immigrants, the United States has around eleven million undocumented immigrants. Europe, which has roughly the same land mass as the United States, has six to fifteen million undocumented immigrants. Immigrants across the world are moving in both directions. Not everyone stays in his or her place of migration. Millions, either willingly or unwillingly, return home each year.

Ruth's Story

The Book of Ruth is a family story of migration, return, and redemption. It opens with Elimelech, his wife Naomi, and their two sons, who took Moabite wives, moving, as migrant workers, to Moab because of a famine. Eventually all the men died, and the women were left alone. Naomi was a stranger in a strange land. She learned that there was no longer famine in Judah, so she exercised her right to return. Ruth, her Moabite daughter-in-law, said, in Ruth 1:16, "Do not press me to leave you or to turn back from following you! Where you go, I will go; where you lodge, I will lodge; your people shall be my people and your God my God!" Naomi returned home. Ruth became the immigrant to Naomi's land. Once there she sought survival for herself and Naomi.

The narrative continued by telling of Boaz's close adherence to God's requirement to offer hospitality to the stranger. First, he told Ruth that he knew all she had done for Naomi since the death of her husband. He stated, "May you have a full reward from the Lord, the God of Israel, under whose wings you have come for refuge!" (Ruth 2:12). Boaz demonstrated his understanding of God's care for the stranger. Ruth responded by thanking Boaz for his hospitality in which she found favor in his sight. He had been kind to her even though she was a stranger. In accord with scriptural instructions to leave sheaves in the field, olives in the trees, and grapes in the vineyard for the aliens, orphans, and widows, Boaz permitted Ruth to glean.

He asked nothing of Ruth but provided for her needs and brought justice through his negotiations for their marriage. Ruth followed Naomi's instructions and visited him on the threshing room floor at night. Boaz offered to redeem and marry her if the closest kinsman was not willing to do so. He was given the right to marry Ruth and brought the undocumented woman into the family. Ruth's marriage to Boaz gave her status in the land. Fortunately for both of them, there were no immigration regulations to complicate their lives. Their marriage could be called a marriage of convenience.

Until recently, undocumented persons in the United States could marry a citizen, file the proper documents, and be legalized. However, laws have changed, and only persons who have entered legally can adjust their status. If they entered with a visa to study, work, visit, or for some other reason and then overstayed and became un-documented, they can marry a citizen and adjust. However, if they crossed a border without documents, it is no longer possible to marry a citizen and adjust status without first returning to their country of origin for a period of up to ten years. Marriages of convenience or for immigration status adjustment are a thing of the past. Couples seeking adjustment of status must pay large fees and pass expensive medical exams and individual examinations on questions about their lives together that prove beyond a doubt that they have married for love and are living together on a daily basis.

Ruth was blessed with finding a good man to marry and care for her, but her circumstances differed from those of many persons seeking to make a living. Often, they are tricked or forced into migrating and discover that they have been sold into slavery. This has been part of the human condition throughout history. In the twenty-first century, men, women, and children are trafficked and brought into the United States and other countries and forced into hard labor, domestic service, and sexual slavery.

Trafficking and Slavery

The biblical migration story includes examples of trafficking and slavery. Jacob had twelve sons. Joseph was his favorite, which caused jealousy among his brothers, who sold him into slavery. He was transported to Egypt where he managed to flourish.

Joseph overcame being a slave. He never forgot that God was with him. The captive slave rose to power as an integral part of the Egyptian government. He had an opportunity to retaliate when famine in his homeland brought his brothers to Egypt seeking grain. Instead of striking back, Joseph offered open, accepting, and forgiving hospitality and welcomed them as though they were strangers, gave them grain, and sent them home. Joseph demonstrated radical forgiveness and the ability to see God in the midst of trials when he said to them in Genesis 45:5, "Do not be distressed, or angry with yourselves, because you sold me here; for God sent me before you to preserve life." It is possible to see the hand of God in the midst of horrendous circumstances. The circle was completed. Joseph invited his family to bring their flocks and possessions to Goshen (Genesis 43–47).

Today, this solution is not possible. Across the world, families would be more than willing to welcome other family members into the fold; however, immigration laws make family reunification difficult. Families wait years and sometimes decades to be reunited. According to the June 2010 U.S. Department of State visa bulletin, the backlogs for family members range from 2.5 to 22 years.[4] Visas depend on country of origin, family relationships, and the family member's status as a citizen or legal permanent resident.

Joseph helped his family escape starvation. Throughout the world, immigration laws do not grant legal status persons because they are starving. Our economy, which needs the migrant workers, who come to feed their families and to feed us, forces them to live undocumented lives and to work in substandard conditions. Some are successful. Others literally die for a job. They work in difficult jobs with no benefits and are unable to afford health care when injured on the job or become too sick to work.

For others, their dreams do not always materialize to the degree envisioned, with 61 percent of U.S. farmworkers' income falling below the poverty level. A median income of less than $7,500 a year leaves many feeling trapped with no options other than farm work and with the shame of returning to their homelands with less than what they came.[5]

Economic conditions are also a major cause of worldwide trafficking. It has historically been an accepted part of many cultures. In the discussion of immigration it is important to note that the

African slaves did not come to this country by choice. They were part of a triangular system of trade known as the Middle Passage. Goods manufactured in Europe were sent to African markets where they were traded for purchased or kidnapped Africans who were enslaved. Once in North America, the slaves were traded or sold for raw materials to be sent to European manufacturers, which would complete the voyage, and the cycle would begin again. This information is crucial to the immigration debate, as it defines the issues and reminds us that we have a special responsibility to the African Americans, as their ancestors' lives were ripped away from them and they were forcibly transported to the United States. We must also realize that many of the slaves readily embraced Christianity because they left Africa as Christians.

One of the first converts we hear about in the Bible was the Ethiopian eunuch, who is placed by scholars as being from an area in present day Sudan (Acts 8:26–40). Early Christianity spread into Africa and spawned many of our church fathers and mothers. St. Augustine, perhaps the most important theological figure in Western Christianity, was born in North Africa. We can only begin to realize how many of our beliefs were formulated in Africa. This makes slavery even more abhorrent. This realization gave us one of the most cherished of all hymns. "Amazing Grace" was born from John Newton's life as captain of a slave ship and his realization that even a "wretch like me" could be the recipient of God's grace and turn his life around.

The African slaves were brought here with the blessings of many a church member. In fact, when one visits Cape Coast Castle in Ghana, which was a port in the Middle Passage, the connection between church and slavery can be readily seen. The Rev. Joe Roberson of Church World Service vividly describes this phenomenon by describing the beautiful church on the shore of the island, which was built on top of a chamber carved in the rocks that had a barred opening for slaves to enter. There was no door on the other side. Rather hundreds of trafficked persons were pushed into the cramped quarters to wait. They had a choice to either wait for the ship to carry them to they knew not where or leave their imprisonment by jumping into the sea and drowning or being eaten by the sharks.

Mr. Roberson describes Sunday mornings on the island: The congregants sang praises and hymns to God's glory while the slaves waited below in inhumane, crowded, unsanitary conditions, with little or no food or water. In his words, "There it was Heaven above and Hell below!" Terrifyingly, it probably never dawned on the worshippers that their actions were in complete contradiction to the teachings of the Christ they were worshipping.

They believed in heaven above and hell below and had no qualms about claiming heaven for themselves and relegating others to hell directly below them. This situation continues today in varying degrees and varying places. *Story shared by Joe Roberson with Church World Service. Included with his permission.*

Many of us are complicit in advancing human trafficking. We look for bargains without ever thinking of the conditions trafficked persons endure so cheap goods are available to the bargain hunters of the world. The need to survive coupled with the desire for cheap labor to increase profits has resulted in the continuation of modern-day slavery or bondage and the trafficking of men, women, and children at many levels. *Trafficking in persons* and *human trafficking* are terms that refer to holding people in involuntary servitude, slavery, debt bondage, and/or forced labor. The majority of human trafficking in the world is in forced labor. The U.S. Department of State's Trafficking in Persons report in 2010 reports that for every person trafficked for prostitution, nine are trafficked for labor. However, women and girls trafficked for labor are often also sexually exploited, which can skew the statistics.[6]

Around the world, 12.3 million adults and children are in forced labor, bonded labor, and forced prostitution. This breaks down to 1.8 trafficking victims for every 1,000 persons worldwide. In Asia and the Pacific, the number is higher. In those regions, there are 3 trafficking victims for every 1,000 inhabitants. Trafficking generates more than 32 billion dollars a year. It is second only to drug trafficking in amount of earned revenue.[7]

The following paragraph is taken from the Country Narrative on the United States from the 2010 Trafficking in Persons Report. The United States is identified by Global Fast as one of the primary destinations for trafficked persons, along with the United States, Italy, Japan, Canada, Australia, and other advanced nations:

> The United States is a source, transit, and destination country for men, women, and children subjected to trafficking in persons, specifically forced labor, debt bondage, and forced prostitution. Trafficking occurs primarily for labor and most commonly in domestic servitude, agriculture, manufacturing, janitorial services, hotel services, construction, health and elder care, hair and nail salons, and strip club dancing. Vulnerabilities remain even for legally documented temporary workers who typically fill labor needs in the hospitality, landscaping, construction, food service, and agricultural industries. In some human trafficking cases, workers are victims of fraudulent recruitment practices and have incurred large debts for promised employment in the United States,

which makes them susceptible to debt bondage and involuntary servitude. More U.S. citizens, both adult and children, are found in sex trafficking than labor trafficking; U.S. citizen child victims are often runaway and homeless youth. More foreign victims are found in labor trafficking than sex trafficking, some of whom have entered the country under work- or student-based visa programs. Primary countries of origin for foreign victims certified by the U.S. government were Thailand, Mexico, Philippines, Haiti, India, Guatemala, and the Dominican Republic. Eighty-two percent of these foreign adult victims and 56 percent of foreign child trafficking victims were labor trafficking victims. Sex trafficking of foreign children included boys.[8]

Linda Smith, founder of Shared Hope International, an organization that works with trafficking victims, says in a Shared Hope International report on sex trafficking, "The market for sex trafficking and sex tourism is just like a shopping mall. Buyers can choose from a variety of human products of various ages and colors, and as long as buyers continue to purchase this human product and facilitators support the market, the shopping mall stays open."[9]

According to Free the Slaves, 800,000 people are trafficked each year globally, with 14,500–17,000 people trafficked into the United States. There are at least 10,000 enslaved persons in the United States on any day, and 50 percent of them are children. There are more slaves now than any time in history, with an estimated 27 million persons enslaved worldwide.[10]

Throughout the world workers are victimized by debt bondage when traffickers exploit the initial debt agreed on for employment. In some areas, people can inherit the debt of their ancestors and be forced to work to pay off those debts. Debt bondage can be seen at times among migrant workers who have acquired the debt in their home countries.

LeeAnn Strine, an advocate for immigrant rights in Central Pennsylvania, worked with a young woman who had been trafficked into the United States. Fourteen-year-old Theresa (not her real name) was from an impoverished family from an African country. An American doctor offered to pay her family to send her to the United States as a housekeeper, nanny, babysitter, and provider of other services needed by him or his family.

He arranged for passports and documents, and on arrival in the United States the doctor handed Theresa's documentation over to a woman who posed as her aunt. Posing as her uncle he enrolled her in school. At that point, the "aunt" disappeared and was never seen again.

Theresa went to school and did very well. After school she did housework and cared for two elementary school-aged girls and eventually a baby, who appeared suddenly. She never knew why or how the baby came to be there. About a year later, the wife had a baby, so Theresa was caring for four children.

The doctor traveled often and would be gone for as much as six months at a time. LeeAnn discerned a great deal of fear on the part of the children and Theresa when he was present, and she suspected sexual abuse.

Theresa met Andrew (not his real name), who was an asylum seeker from the same country and was attracted to her. He made arrangements for his family to pay the doctor for the privilege of dating her, which meant she would move in with him and become his property.

She desperately wanted out of the doctor's house and was infatuated with Andrew. LeeAnn helped Theresa move out, but not before the doctor informed her of all he had done for her and letting her know if she left she would be a persona non grata and would never be able to return to his house. He also let LeeAnn know that he should be getting more money for the girl.

Up to this point, every person in Theresa's life had abandoned her or used her as a negotiating tool for services or money. No one had had her well-being at heart or had asked her what she wanted. In her mind, she really did owe the doctor; if not for him she would not be where she was. She never understood that she had been used and abused. This was simply the way things were.

Theresa moved in with Andrew and they were living happily. They had two children and were planning their wedding when he was killed in an accident. Theresa was determined to complete her education and make a home for her children. She sent the children to Africa while she finished school. At this time, the children have returned and been reunited with their mother. Theresa is a legal resident and working mom and is looking forward to the day she becomes a U.S. citizen. *From personal communication with Lee Ann Strine, immigration advocate, York, Pennsylvania.*

Domestic workers are often in situations of involuntary servitude. They are very often isolated and forced into relationships of sexual abuse resulting in untreated illnesses. Because many of them work in private homes it is often difficult to discover them or inspect their living conditions.

The exploitation of children is perhaps the worst type of trafficking. Children are sold for labor and sex. They are also forced to be child soldiers or sexual partners for the military. UNICEF states that as many as one million children enter the multibillion dollar commercial sex trade each year.[11] Child soldiers are often forced to do unthinkable things. One teen who was trying to reenter society in his homeland told a case worker, "I killed my mother and raped my sister. Is it possible for God to love me? What do you think? Should I be punished? Have I been punished enough?"[12] This is the reality of the horror with which he lives. Will he ever be able to restore his life to some semblance of normal?

While working with a group of young women asylum seekers from Burma, I learned that they routinely endured rape by the military. When they went into the forest to collect firewood for daily cooking, if a soldier saw them and chose to rape them, there was nothing they could do to prevent the rape. When I asked if they reported the rapes, they said no, they just sat by the side of the road and cried a bit and then went home and said nothing. Rape was the norm. At that time, men could buy licenses to rape in their country. The women had managed to get tourists visas and had fled to a U.S. territory and sought asylum. It was very difficult for young women to get permission to leave Burma. They told me it was because the government wanted them to remain in Burma so they could be trafficked within their own country.

Women make up 56 percent of the persons trafficked across the world and 70 percent of those trafficked from Indonesia. They are pushed out of developing countries because of economic, social, and family conditions and are vulnerable to slavery. They find themselves performing cheap, compliant labor in brothels, factories, fisheries, fields, and service industries.

Esther's Story

The Book of Esther is an example of exploitation and trafficking of women. First the exploitation: Queen Vashti was ordered by the king, who "was merry with wine," to appear at a large banquet he was holding for all of his officials. He ordered her to appear wearing her royal crown (and according to the Aramaic translation of the Old Testament, only her crown) so all might see how beautiful she was. Queen Vashti refused. The king realized this would tempt the women of the land to begin to refuse orders, so he had Queen Vashti banished forever. He sent letters declaring that every man should be master of his own house. He then realized that he had lost his queen. In response to his being without a queen, we see what has the appearance of trafficking.

Men were sent throughout the kingdom to "gather all the beautiful young virgins" so the king might choose a replacement for Queen Vashti. Esther (Hadassah) was beautiful and had been adopted by Mordecai. He permitted her to be taken to the king's palace.

Mordecai instructed Esther not to tell of her Jewish heritage and visited her every day. She eventually became Queen Vashti's replacement and very important in Jewish history. Haman, a court official, planned to destroy all Jews in the kingdom. Mordecai begged Esther to ask the king for her life and the lives of all the Jews.

Although Esther had not been called in to see the king for almost a month, she fasted and prayed for three days in preparation for making an uninvited visit to the king. All the Jews joined in fasting and praying. After three days, although not summoned, Esther went to the throne room and approached the king. She was well received and invited the king and Haman to a banquet where she disclosed that she was a Jew and asked that her people be spared.

The story ended favorably for the Jews. Esther's request was granted, and Haman was executed. Mordecai was promoted to Haman's position, and the Jews were delivered. The Jews celebrate Purim each year in remembrance of this. The holiday's name is derived from Haman's casting lots or "pur" to choose the date of the Jews destruction.

Once again, we see God bringing good from evil. A harsh reality is the knowledge that God does bring good from evil, but there are also moments when the good does not seem to come and evil triumphs. We often ask why or why not? We might also ask, are there situations of evil that continue because we choose to not take the radically inclusive hospitable path of Christ and instead take only the first step of praying about a situation without realizing that, whenever possible, we are to actively work for God's Kin-dom to come on earth? Do we see injustices and stand silently by when our actions might be what is needed to stop the injustice? Italian poet Dante said, "The hottest places in hell are reserved for those who in times of great moral crises choose neutrality." Neutrality may be a safe place to be, but often it is where we can ignore our faith teachings and the crisis at hand.

Esther was living in a time of crisis. She fasted and prayed, as did her people, but she did not stop there. She then took action. It is at the point of action that we become real. In Isaiah 58:6–10 God speaks of the type of fasting that is required:

> Is not this the fast that I choose: to loose the bonds of injustice, to undo the thongs of the yoke, to let the oppressed go free, and to break every yoke? Is it not to share your bread with the hungry, and bring the homeless poor into your house; when you see the naked, to cover them, and not to hide yourself from your own kin? Then your light shall break forth like the dawn, and your healing shall spring up quickly; your vindicator shall go before you, the glory of the Lord shall be your rearguard. Then you shall call, and the Lord will answer; you shall cry for help, and he will say, Here I am. If you remove the yoke from among you, the pointing of the finger, the speaking of evil, if you offer your food to the hungry and satisfy

the needs of the afflicted, then your light shall rise in the darkness and your gloom be like the noonday.

Prayer for Change

Had Esther stopped with prayer and fasting, we would not know her story, and many of her people would have died. Many of us are called to pray, to fast, and to act. Others, because of our life's condition or physical condition are called to only pray or to fast. In Esther's story, others were acting in harmony with her. They were dependent on one another. We are also aware of the power of prayer. There is a Chinese Buddhist sect that highly reveres the elderly who are recognized for their power of meditation and prayer. Seniors are moved into special housing that enables them to spend their days in meditation and prayer for the greater community. They are known for their wisdom, power, and the good that they do. Growing old is considered a welcome blessing—not a curse.

Our seniors are an untapped reservoir of strength and power. Just imagine what would happen if we valued the power of prayer as highly as physical capabilities. The elderly could change our world for the better. We have all experienced the power of prayer. As a nation, what would happen if we called on the seniors and those who are unable to take physical action to pray simply for change in our land for God's will to be done in solving our problems? Praying for God's will takes us out of the equation. It says, your will is important, God, not mine.

Immigration is, for many, a hot-button issue. It would be a hot button issue for Jesus, who came that God's will be done. As people of faith, seeking to learn as much as we can about immigration and to do the right thing and offer radical hospitality, one thing we can immediately agree on is that to pray for God's will without telling God what that will should be is always the right thing to do. This prayer does not require taking sides. We can be in total disagreement and be unified in praying that God's will be done. Then all we have to do is sit back and wait. With patience, we will learn the answer and see the actions that brought it about by all praying the same prayer and, when able, acting on the issue.

In Joseph's case, without a doubt, he fasted, prayed, and acted. He took advantage of the situation into which he was thrust. He took action and did not hold a grudge. Rather, he forgave and was able to give life to himself and his family. Both Joseph and Esther were victims of trafficking, and both rose above their situation and brought about the greater good. However, there are others, millions of others, who are waiting for us to act to bring God's Kin-dom on earth here and now.

As Christians we are called to take steps to bring an end to injustice. Living as radical, inclusive, hospitable followers of Christ, we are called to remember the letter to the Colossians 3:10–11 where we are reminded that we "have clothed yourselves with the new self, which is being renewed in knowledge according to the image of its creator. In that renewal there is no longer Greek and Jew, circumcised and uncircumcised, barbarian, Scythian, slave and free; but Christ is all and in all!"

Unfortunately we have ignored this scripture or have been selective in its application. In order for radical, inclusive, hospitable theology to take hold, it is necessary to confess our sin of exclusivity as a nation and covenant for inclusivity. *As a nation* is the key phrase, because many people are truly open to welcoming the stranger but have not had the opportunity to do so. It is time for those who are open to the strangers to speak out, to become advocates for immigrants, migrants, refugees, asylum seekers, and the ancestors of the victims of the Middle Passage as well as all persons being trafficked today. We must let our friends, families, churches, and governing officials know that we are ready to begin ministries that build hospitable communities open to every person God puts in our path and our neighborhood.

What Would Jesus Do?

The immigration question directly relates to the racism question. Just as there were and are Christians who embraced slavery, there are Christians who embrace anti-immigrant sentiments and actions. For balance, the question to always ask is, "What would Jesus do?" Would Jesus own slaves? Would Jesus care more about getting a bargain in the marketplace than laborers getting fair wages? Would Jesus traffic children, women, or men? Would Mary Magdelene or any of the women around Jesus frequent a nail salon knowing that the women worked for tips only? Would Jesus insist on being served the best and first? Would Jesus turn away from any human being? Would Jesus, the son of God, consider himself superior to any person? The questions can go on and on. The next question is, what would we do? If a stranger moved in near Jesus, what would he do? If a stranger moves in near us, what would we do? What is the Holy Spirit telling us to do?

Are we and our churches open to all people? If not, we are practicing the sin of exclusivity. In order to confess the sin of exclusivity, it is necessary look at the historic treatment of black sisters and brothers because that treatment continues today and includes Hispanics, Middle Easterners, and others who have become the victims of acceptable social, political, ethnic, racial, and religious abuse.

In *The Arrogance of Faith*, Forrest Wood explains, "One can say that, good works notwithstanding, there has been no greater religious force in the dehumanization of humans than Christianity, the self-proclaimed religion of peace, brotherly love, and fellowship."[13] The arrogance of Christianity is that there are many who profess Christianity but who do not rejoice in diversity, and they are very vocal with their voices and their votes. The Christians who blessed slavery did so because in their heart of hearts they believed that white supremacy was the true religion. The Christian who is presently working to eliminate migrants, immigrants, refugees, and asylum seekers from our country continues to practice Christianity of white supremacy.

From 2000 to 2008, the number of hate groups in the United States grew by 54 percent. According to the Southern Poverty Law Center (SPLC), the increase resulted from immigration fears, a failing economy, and Barack Obama being elected president. The SPLC identified 926 hate groups in 2008, up more than 4 percent from the 888 groups in 2007 and far above the 602 groups documented in 2000.[14]

However, no true followers of Christ believe in white supremacy because to believe that one group is superior to another is to deny Jesus who welcomed all and God who created us male and female of many colors. Joining a group that claims superiority over another group is stepping away from Christ's teachings.

Ethnic Inequities

In the United States, blacks have been held captive by a socioeconomic system that refuses to let them become a part of the supposed democratic system that keeps them "in their place." This has been successfully done, while an image has been perpetrated that claims things have changed since the civil rights events of the 1960s. In 2011, the Pew Research Center analyzed 2009 government data and discovered that the median wealth of white households was 20 times that of black households and 18 times that of Hispanic households.[15] The ethnic group economic gap continues to widen. The National Poverty Center statistics show that in 2010 the overall poverty rate for the United States was 14.4 percent. Among groups, poverty affected 27.4 percent of blacks, 26.6 percent of Hispanics, and 24.3 percent of Native Americans. Noncitizens had a poverty rate of 26.7 percent.[16]

The images of horrific poverty that followed in the wake of Hurricane Katrina in 2005 opened the eyes of much of the country about poverty in the United States. Blacks were denied overall economic growth. Legislation is being passed to eliminate entry of other people of color who might be coming to our shores.

Some Christians assume they have divine authority. They do not welcome the stranger and demand Americanization or deportation. As a country whose identity lies in a multicultural milieu, many people demand that anyone who does not fit into the prevailing white American image either do so or risk permanent alienation and rejection. We forget that every person's identity is tied up in language, customs, and ancestry. The New Testament makes it very clear that all persons and cultures are acceptable, and we should never risk any action that might negatively impact another person's search for Christ.

The United States, as a nation of immigrants, has the potential to be open to the inclusive Christ who can heal the wounds of very diverse people. Both the citizens and the residents (without regard to status and ethnicity) need this healing. It may come from the realization that the downward spiral of the country and the churches may be a result of the great majority of Christians refusing to respond to the 1960s' Civil Rights Movement. We must apologize for that sin and repent, welcome and embrace black brothers and sisters into full communion in the community of God. In the same respect, as people of color, we must be willing to accept the apology and move forward. We must, on all sides, confess the sin of exclusivity—as it moves in all directions—and repent for the harm that has been done. We must learn that if we are to be Christians (of any color) we must embrace the stranger. Not only must we embrace the stranger, we must realize that the stranger is first and foremost made in the image of God and we are each the stranger to the person we see as the stranger.

It is our responsibility to admit to and to repent sins of exclusion, oppression, prejudice, and bias. It is up to us to ask forgiveness and to seek new ways to embrace the diversity of the stranger. We must be willing to understand that our comfort zones can be a form of unintended exclusivity that pits one group of people against another and perpetrates the myth of superiority or the myth that our way is the only right way. Certain interpretations of Christianity are against the grain of the gospel. These myths are the underlying problems of many of our country's and Christianity's major dilemmas. They cannot be solved by relegating whole ethnic groups to ghettos or by closing borders and shutting out immigrants.

We must erase the myths by seeing and welcoming Christ who is standing with the strangers and with us. Prejudices have taken hold because Christians have endorsed them. The ultimate reality is that immigrants are the manifested God, and God has been shut out of many of our churches. Ironically, the majority of immigrants are Christians, and even they are often not welcomed. However, churches that welcome immigrants are experiencing church growth and new life.

Who Will We Welcome?

The time has arrived to decide if we are going to welcome the radical, inclusive, hospitable, and very diverse God into our churches or if we are going to replace the Trinitarian concept of a diverse community with the sterile idol of a brightly polished golden cross with a Jesus who prefers one group of people over the other. How far, we must ask ourselves, is the golden cross of today from the golden calf of ancient Israel?

If we continue to isolate all but the presently dominant race instead of incorporating our various cultures into a diversified and honored multicultural society and church, we will be saving our world for ourselves and leaving our God, who migrates, behind. Try as some of us might to stop migration, it will continue. Immigrants have gradually changed the face of this continent since the first explorers set foot in North America. Until the twenty-first century, with the exception of the Middle Passage, the great majority of immigrants were of European descent. They had the same general appearance and came from the same continent. However, each ethnic and religious group experienced prejudices and discrimination. As each integrated into the land, the established citizens often discriminated against the next group that arrived.

Although many undocumented immigrants of European ethnicity live in the United States, their faces have been ignored in the immigration debate; rather, the media and the general public have chosen to concentrate on the Hispanic population, which is readily identifiable and targeted for anti-immigrant sentiments. We cannot help but note that although prejudice against African Americans, which was once tolerated and encouraged, has, at least on the surface, become politically incorrect, it has become very acceptable to discriminate against certain groups of immigrants, especially Hispanic and Middle Eastern immigrants. In addition, undocumented immigrants are relegated to a subservient class without the rights and privileges of other children of God.

In 1774, in "Thoughts Upon Slavery," John Wesley offered wisdom that continues to be applicable today:

> If, therefore, you have any regard to justice (to say nothing of mercy, nor the revealed law of God), render unto all their due. Give liberty to whom liberty is due, that is, to every child of man, to every partaker of human nature.

Let none serve you but by his own act and deed, by his own voluntary choice. Away with all whips, all chains, all compulsion! Be gentle toward all men; and see that you invariably do unto every one as you would he should do unto you.[17]

Wesley rephrased the Golden Rule, which can be found in all of the world's great religions. These thoughts can easily be transferred to today's immigration situation, where we find immigrants and migrants working in undesirable conditions and often suffering from being trafficked and literally enslaved in subhuman conditions. As followers of Christ it is important to embrace Psalm 82:3–4 and "give justice to the weak and the orphan; maintain the right of the lowly and the destitute. Rescue the weak and the needy; deliver them from the hand of the wicked." Theologically, by offering radical, inclusive hospitality, we are following the Golden Rule and doing to others what we would have done to us.

Notes

1. Eric Weiner and Lindsay Mangum, "Debunking Global Migration Myths," National Public Radio, June 6, 2007, www.npr.org/templates/story/story.php?storyId=10767136.
2. World Bank, "Topics in Development: Migration & Remittances," July 2011, http://go.worldbank.org/RR8SDPEHO0.
3. Weiner and Mangum, "Debunking Global Migration Myths."
4. U.S. Department of State, "Visa Bulletin for June 2010," http://travel.state.gov/visa/bulletin/bulletin_4879.html.
5. Eduardo Gonzalez Jr., "Migrant Farmworkers: Our Nation's Invisible Population," May 27, 2008, www.extension.org/pages/9960/migrant-farm-workers:-our-nations-invisible-population.
6. U.S. Department of State, "Trafficking in Persons Report 2010," www.state.gov/g/tip/rls/tiprpt/2010.
7. Ibid.

8. U.S. Department of State, "Trafficking in Persons Report 2010: Country Narratives, Countries N–Z," www.state.gov/g/tip/rls/tiprpt/2010/142761.htm.

9. Glory Dharmaraj, "Human Trafficking Awareness and Action: A Bible Study," January 7, 2011, www.unitedmethodistwomen.org/resources/articles/item/index.cfm?id=355.

10. Free the Slaves, "About Slavery FAQ," www.freetheslaves.net/SSLPage.aspx?pid=304.

11. UNICEF Convention on the Rights of the Child, "Optional Protocol on the Sale of Children, Child Prostitution and Child Pornography," Updated June 2, 2011, www.unicef.org/crc/index_30204.html.

12. Personal communication with immigration attorney who wishes to remain anonymous.

13. Forrest G. Wood, *The Arrogance of Faith: Christianity and Racism in America* (New York: Alfred A. Knopf, 1991), 12.

14. David Holthouse, "The Year in Hate," *Intelligence Report* 133 (Spring 2009), www.splcenter.org/get-informed/intelligence-report/browse-all-issues/2009/spring/the-year-in-hate. See also the Leadership Conference, "Confronting the New Faces of Hate: Hate Crimes in America 2009," www.civilrights.org/publications/hatecrimes/white-supremacist.html.

15. Rakesh Kochhar, Richard Fry, and Paul Taylor, "The Toll of the Great Recession: Hispanic Household Wealth Fell by 66% from 2005 to 2009," Pew Rearch Center, July 26, 2011, www.pewhispanic.org/2011/07/26/the-toll-of-the-great-recession.

16. National Poverty Center, "Poverty in the United States: Frequently Asked Questions," www.npc.umich.edu/poverty.

17. John Wesley, "Thoughts Upon Slavery," General Board of Global Ministries, http://new.gbgm-umc.org/umhistory/wesley/slavery.

Chapter 6
Migration and the New Testament

But I say to you that listen, Love your enemies, do
good to those who hate you, bless those who curse
you, pray for those who abuse you.... Be merciful, just
as your Father is merciful.

—Luke 6:27, 36

The New Testament begins with a migration story, as Jesus travels from heaven to earth to be incarnated as a marginalized child of a teen mother who was unwed at his conception. He took the form of a human being and became the refugee, migrant, and, at times, undocumented Christ of our salvation. Near the beginning of Jesus' life, Mary and Joseph fled with him to Egypt as refugees. At the end of his life, he was crucified outside the gates of the city because he did not have the documents of a Roman citizen (Roman citizens were not crucified). He was undocumented. He was a radically inclusive, peaceful, and hospitable messiah who ignored boundaries and welcomed all into his circles of love.

Jesus' Story

Jesus was born in Bethlehem, where his parents had traveled to adhere to King Herod's taxation decree. Tradition holds that the

Christ child was born in a manger, a stable, a shed like the children of many of today's migrants who are born along the road as their parents seek work and a place to call home.

The news of Jesus' birth was given first to shepherds, the lowest group on the social scale. They were migrants, who moved and lived with their flocks while doing seasonal work. It was also given to "Magi," who were probably astrologers, magicians or sorcerers from Persia, Babylon, or Arabia. They traveled to Jerusalem seeking the "child who has been born King of the Jews." The Bible does not indicate that there were three Magi or that they were kings. In fact, in Matthew 2:1 they are called "wise men from the East."* The term "Magi" comes from the same root as "magic" and "magicians." Such persons (Daniel 2:2) watched the stars, were able to predict solar and lunar eclipses, and attempted to predict events to come. Strangers/foreigners/astrologers from afar read the stars and identified the messiah. In fact, they followed a star that they may have worshipped. That star taught them the truth of the Christ child. We might say the wise men were the first converts to a belief in Jesus.

Luke's gospel tells us that the holy family stayed in Bethlehem until Mary and Joseph took Jesus to the temple in Jerusalem to be dedicated. They then returned to Nazareth (Luke 2:22–39). Matthew records that they stayed in Bethlehem until the Magi's visit when Jesus was about two years old. After the Magi left,

> an angel of the Lord appeared to Joseph in a dream and said, "Get up, take the child and his mother, and flee to Egypt, and remain there until I tell you; for Herod is about

---

* Astrologers, or "wisemen" ("magoi" in Greek): literate, political officials in the courts of Parthis, Armenia, or regions east of Judea. Foreign regimes often sent emissaries to greet and give gifts to new kings or rulers. The visit highlights the conflict between the king of Israel chosen by God (Jesus) and the king of Israel chosen by the Romans (Herod). See Michael D. Coogan, ed., *The New Oxford Annotated Bible*, 3rd Edition, NRSV (New York: Oxford University Press, 2001).

to search for the child, to destroy him." Then Joseph got up, took the child and his mother by night, and went to Egypt, and remained there until the death of Herod. This was to fulfill what had been spoken by the Lord through the prophet, "Out of Egypt I have called my son." (Matthew 2:13–15)

Jesus, Mary, and Joseph became asylum-seeking refugees in Egypt. Without travel documents, they crossed the border, looking for safety and sanctuary. Although they were strangers, someone welcomed them and protected them. Keeping ethnicity in mind, to have hidden in Egypt, the holy family would have had to look very much like the Egyptians. This would be very different from traditional images of the holy family. Perhaps it is time to embrace the ethnicity of the holy family and all people of the Bible.

Meanwhile, in Bethlehem, Herod planned to find and kill Jesus. When he discovered the Magi had left without divulging the child's location, he ordered the killing of all children in the area who were two years old and under (Matthew 2:16).

Jesus and his family fled political, religious, and ethnic persecution. These are all present-day grounds for asylum and refugee status. However, if the holy family arrived at a U.S. border before 2010, it is probable that Jesus would have been sent to a children's detention center and then foster care, Mary to a women's detention center, and Joseph to a men's detention center. (Although there were and are a few family detention centers, there are not enough to serve the needs of all families who are part of the migrating population.)

Unaccompanied children can live through nightmares while waiting for help. A three-year-old Guatemalan indigenous child is one such example. She was questioned for two days by

Immigration and Customs Enforcement (ICE) officers. ICE complained to the pro-bono attorney assigned to the case that the child was not cooperating and would not answer their simple questions. She would not even give them her name and address. ICE was outraged that all she would say was no. After two days the little girl was hysterical. They could not understand why she would not speak to them, as they were speaking to her in Spanish. It never occurred to them that as an indigenous child the little girl didn't speak Spanish or English. Intervention from Kids in Need of Defense (KIND) had the child taken to a hospital to be treated, to calm down, to rest, and to interact with someone who spoke her language. *From personal communication with immigration attorney who wishes to remain anonymous.*

In the United States each member of the holy family would be required to secure his or her own legal help or to plead his or her case for asylum. Asylum seekers are routinely detained and do not receive legal help from the government. There is a large network of pro-bono legal organizations, such as Justice for Our Neighbors (JFON), which was developed by the United Methodist Committee on Relief (UMCOR); Kids in Need of Defense (KIND); and Human Rights First. Unfortunately the number of asylum seekers, migrants, immigrants, and refugees in need of pro-bono legal assistance greatly outpaces the help that is available.

JFON asylum cases have included seeking asylum for women from Jamaica and Colombia. They included a former Jamaican police officer and mother of two minor children who fled to the United States in the wake of a high profile extradition of a drug dealer.

It was alleged that she blew the whistle on police corruption. She asked for asylum based on a credible fear of persecution should she be returned to her country. Her life was in danger. Another case was a mother from Colombia and her thirteen-year-old daughter who sought asylum based on domestic violence. Domestic violence has no boundaries and is a worldwide problem that can, at times, be the basis for an asylum claim. *From personal communication with Thomas J. Mills, Justice for Our Neighbors employee.*

We don't know what happened to the holy family in Egypt, However, we can surmise that they were welcomed, made a living (with or without documents), and after the death of Herod, were able to return to their home in the town of Nazareth.

We hear very little about Jesus until he begins his ministry by reading from Isaiah 61, "The Spirit of the Lord is upon me, because he has anointed me to bring good news to the poor. He has sent me to proclaim release to the captives and recovery of sight to the blind, to let the oppressed go free, to proclaim the year of the Lord's favor" (Luke 4:18). Jesus was ushering in a new era of love for all.

Matthew 4:13 explains that eventually Jesus left Nazareth and made his home in Capernaum by the sea. He did, at one time, have a home base. From there he began to call men and women to follow him. With his disciples, he migrated throughout the area, often going to the other and the other side as he reached out to all of God's people without regard to their social status, ethnicity, or religion. His cross-cultural lifestyle had roots in the teachings of the Hebrew sacred texts that called for radical, inclusive hospitality to strangers, widows, and orphans as well as all beings and required feeding, clothing, and taking care of them as the method of worship required by God.

In Luke 9:58, Jesus says, "The foxes have holes, and the birds of the air have nests; but the Son of Man has nowhere to lay his head."[†] Throughout his life, Jesus was moving. He called his disciples to leave what they were doing and to follow him. However, if Jesus and the twelve disciples tried to enter the United States today without proper documents identifying them as citizens of Israel (which Jesus would probably not be able to get because of his political and theological actions), they would be stereotyped as Middle Easterners and either be the victims of expedited removal, which means they would be immediately returned to their point of origin, or they would, most probably, be put in immigration detention.[‡]

Jesus was quite active in supporting the people most in need. He readily saw the plight of the day laborers and resonated with their need to make a living. Most notable is Matthew 20:1–16. In it he likens the kingdom of heaven to a landowner who hires laborers for his vineyard. He hires workers throughout the day who have continued to wait in the marketplace in hopes of employment and pays them all equally at the end of the day, without regard to numbers of hours worked. Finally, when questioned about his actions by those who have worked all day, he reminds them of his right to do what he chooses with what belongs to him and asks, "Or are you envious

---

[†] This is the migrant's story. Like Jesus, who had a home in Capernaum but often no place to lay his head because of his travels, today's migrants often have homes in their countries but often no place to lay their heads in the country to which they have migrated.

[‡] They were thirteen Middle Eastern men. They had no specific home. They moved from place to place and often interacted with stigmatized communities. They went away into the mountains and across the lakes. They were suspected of trying to mobilize the masses against the government. It is not known how they supported themselves, and, at times, they met in rented rooms. Large crowds followed them, and the religious and political communities thought they were instigating uprisings of the masses of the poorest of the poor. On arriving in the United States, they would be part of the targeted list of high-level terrorism suspects.

because I am generous?" He then summarizes what he does with "the last will be first and the first will be last." Jesus understood the plight of the day workers and the scriptural mandate to treat them fairly. He was well versed in scriptures and in paying the workers; he was following the commands of Deuteronomy 24:14–15:

> You shall not withhold the wages of poor and needy laborers, whether other Israelites or aliens who reside in your land in one of your towns. You shall pay them their wages daily before sunset, because they are poor and their livelihood depends on them; otherwise they might cry to the Lord against you, and you would incur guilt.

He was also actively embracing the teachings of scriptures as reflected in Malachi 3:5 against oppressing the hired workers in their wages. The fair treatment of day laborers can also be seen in Leviticus 19:13, "You shall not defraud your neighbor; you shall not steal; and you shall not keep for yourself the wages of a laborer until morning."

Jesus knew the scriptures very well. It is not difficult to imagine Jesus standing among the day laborers on any city street looking for work and welcome. Employers who hire day laborers and undocumented workers are reminded of the biblical mandate to care for the stranger because he or she might be Christ in disguise. It may be a moment in our lives when the stranger/refugee/migrant may very well be Christ in a "distressing disguise," as Mother Teresa described some of the people she served.[1] Would any of us want to cheat Jesus out of a just wage? Anyone hired must be treated justly and paid fairly.

The importance of fair treatment of workers throughout the Bible is the basis for followers of Christ becoming involved in immigration reform and viewing migrant workers as sisters and brothers. Bill

Mefford, director of civil and human rights for the General Board of Church and Society of The United Methodist Church, states:

> Our goal is to build long-term sustainable movements among United Methodists defending the rights of immigrants. The movement we are building is entirely based on incarnational relationships with immigrant communities. From a position of incarnation, people of faith can move from mercy to justice, from activism to organizing. Incarnation provides the only way to know and share in the stories and voices of immigrants who are regularly being marginalized and oppressed. Only from standing in solidarity can we attain genuine justice for immigrants. And only from an incarnational position with immigrants, advocating for justice and dignity, can we truly call ourselves a movement for the rights of immigrants.[2]

The Korean Community Church in Englewood, New Jersey, is a United Methodist congregation with an outreach to Hispanic day laborers. As Steve Chung drove past the day laborers lined up on the street each day, "Whatever you did for the least of these brothers of mine, you did for me" kept coming into his mind. Being an immigrant from Korea, Mr. Chung felt a kinship with the migrant workers. He prayed for one hundred days and God let him know that the day laborers were all angels. With that knowledge, Street Angels ministry was born.

Four days a week, two church vans pick up between fifteen and thirty Hispanic laborers. They are taken to the church and fed a hot meal, given an opportunity to participate in a Spanish

Bible study, and then take classes for job training in electronics, construction, computers, refrigeration, or English.

Mr. Chung says, "We understand the immigrants because we are immigrants." The ministry requires the work of fifty volunteers and is a sanctuary for the immigrants. Almost every one of them is undocumented. The local police chief has no problem with the Street Angel program and blames the federal government for the immigration problems, not the workers who are simply trying to make a better life for themselves.

"What we do is based on the law of God," says Mr. Chung. "I think the law of God is much, much higher than the law of the world." *From "Korean Congregation Serves Hispanic/Latino 'Street Angels'" by James Melchiorre, United Methodist News Service, December 13, 2006.*

Jesus came to bring a new commandment, a commandment of love of all people. He taught love of God, neighbor, and oneself, and he added a completely new radical and inclusive thought— a completely new teaching: "Love your enemy." He commanded us to love all people. In Luke 6:27-28 and 36 Jesus explains, "But I say to you that listen, Love your enemies, do good to those who hate you, bless those who curse you, pray for those who abuse you. . . . Be merciful, just as your Father is merciful." In other words, we are to follow Christ's teachings and live in ways that reflect his love and God's love by offering radical, inclusive hospitality to everyone we meet.

There is no room in Christ's teachings for a "them and us" mentality. In Matthew 25:40, he clearly states that all, including people who might be seen as the "least of these," are members of his family. As we consider ourselves members of his family, obviously we are all in this together and called to care for one another.

Pastor John Schmidt knew *cielo azul* meant blue sky, but it was welcome news to him that *cielo* also meant heaven. He felt the name was very fitting for a one and a half acre plot of ground on the property of the Santa Rosa Alliance Church in Santa Rosa, California. The triangular plot would be the site of Cielo Azul Farm, a community garden that brings together the efforts of Santa Rosa Alliance Church, St. Joseph Health System, and day laborers.

The planned garden would provide day laborers and their families with extra wages. The St. Joseph Health System had a hiring system for day laborers that guaranteed a minimum of twelve dollars an hour for those workers who participated in an orderly hiring process. Then the economy crashed. Construction work, home improvement, and frequent yard work all began to dry up. Work was hard to find.

Santa Rosa Alliance Church provided land and a solution. The land became a farm and a threefold project. The farm generates income for the men and women involved, families have access to fresh healthy vegetables, and it gives back to the community.

Cielo Azul is also building relationships with local community clinics that will allow them to sell their produce at the health center. The workers came up with the name. They called it Cielo Azul Farm, using the English *farm* rather than the Spanish *granja* because they wanted to reach out to the English-speaking population.

The interaction of people from different populations allows them to learn from and get to know one another. With these interactions, hearts open, minds open, and doors open as all stand in solidarity with the Christ in the vineyard. They are aware that everyone is their neighbor and work together in community. *From "Church Garden Offers Hand to Day Laborers" by Martin Espinoza,* Jonalero News, *March 29, 2010.*

The Good Samaritan

In Luke 10:29, when a lawyer asked Jesus, "Who is my neighbor?" Jesus responded with the parable of the Good Samaritan (Luke 10:29–37), who was on a journey and came upon a man who had been badly beaten and was in need of help. The religious leaders, the priest and the Levite (his designated lay associate), passed by because touching the wounded outsider would make them unclean. However, when the Samaritan saw the beaten man, he felt compassion and cared for him. The Samaritan was not a citizen of that territory. His presence was not welcomed, and yet he, the stranger, helped the victim of the robbery. He showed compassion and acted in love toward a person who would very probably have considered him an enemy. For this act he became known throughout history as the Good Samaritan.

The question remains, just who was the man who had been beaten? Perhaps the most intriguing idea is that he was Jesus. In helping the unknown man lying dying in the dirt, it is very possible that the Samaritan reached out and touched God. He responded without regard to race, religion, ethnicity, membership in a particular social group, or political opinion. He was, unknowingly living a Christ-like life.

Welcoming immigrants provides an opportunity for functioning as modern day Good Samaritans. The Good Samaritan showed love and in giving it also recruited the help of the innkeeper. We are called to show love and to recruit the help of others to become a part of a radical, inclusive hospitable community and to enable others to go and do likewise. Following Jesus leads us into lives of service with and for others.

Jesus' life was a life of service to others, without regard for their national origins or status. His service to strangers can be seen in Luke 17:11–19 with the healing of the lepers. Ten are made clean, but only one comes back. In verse 17–18, when only the foreigner returns, Jesus asked, "Were not ten made clean? But the other nine, where are they? Was none of them found to return and give praise to God except this foreigner?" Jesus offered his healing love to all. We are called to do the same.

Jesus was the ultimate host; he gave himself for the whole world. He demonstrated his radical, inclusive hospitality repeatedly. However, two of those events most clearly demonstrate his selflessness. To the woman at the well, a stranger and outcast, he offered himself as living water and said, "But those who drink of the water that I will give them will never be thirsty" (John 4:14). The Samaritan woman embraced the grace given by Jesus and returned to the city to say to the people, "Come and see a man who told me everything I have ever done! He cannot be the Messiah, can he?" (29).

Many people in that city believed because of her words. The woman at the well was among the very first to spread the good news about Jesus. She was a recipient of Jesus' radical, inclusive hospitality. He was as open to women as to men without regard to cultural and religious traditions. Jesus accepted the woman for exactly who she was. He asked nothing of her but offered his presence, his grace, and his life-giving water of salvation. Although she was not a Jew, he identified himself as the messiah to come, once again repeating his pattern of reaching out to those outside his faith and ethnic and gender group by telling a woman to share his message.

Developing Hospitable Communities

As we seek to offer radical hospitality to all, we must remember that important to the inclusion of immigrants and refugees into community is the intent to keep everyone's cultural and ancestral identities intact and move forward as a diverse yet unified hospitable community. This theology embraces present-day theologies of the developed and developing worlds and segments of traditional Western theology that embrace the teachings of Jesus and facilitate the development of a freeing theology of radical hospitality for the developed world. This theology is developing both inside and outside of the inner circles of organized religion, just as Christ worked outside the inner circles of organized religion. It builds on inclusivity, creativity, and extreme love of one another. It will spread from each of us, who are the stranger to the stranger with Christ in the center as facilitator. We must realize that to each person we see as the stranger, we are seen as the stranger. This meshed theology will draw the scattered and alienated parts of God's community together so it can grow on earth.

Success depends on creating communities that join forces to practice a theology that will be understood by and touch the hearts of masses of people. It must be so basic that it can create the same response in very diverse groups of people. That response is the desire to take the words, actions, and teachings of Jesus seriously. It is a theology of love for one another and the stranger as well as love of the perceived enemy. The term *perceived* is used because we are all sisters and brothers even though we often perceive one another as enemies. Much of this perception is based on physical appearances and media descriptions that divide groups according to ethnicity or class.

The reality is that no matter how physically different two people are, they have more in common than they have differences. Each human being wants to love and be loved, to have the basic necessities of life, to care for loved ones, and to live in and be an integral part of a community. In addition, the Creator God made each and every one of us unique. We can be identified by our physical characteristics. We blend more with similar ethnic groups, but we are who we are because we are each made in the image of God. It is only by embracing this fact that we can truly see God. Radical hospitality enables us to realize that the rainbow of the entire world's people is the image of God. Radical hospitality honors diversity through community. Each person is accepted, respected, welcomed, and embraced for his or her uniqueness, which reflects Christ's uniqueness.

As this new form of hospitality spreads, new communities will form in which not a single person will lose his or her identity. In these communities, the face of the stranger becomes the face of the Christ, and the stranger is valued as Christ just as the stranger is valued by Christ. We are all strangers building new community together. We are all humbled at the thought that Christ is to be seen in each and every one of us.

This coming together of people will include all who have come to a realization of the historical and cultural oppression and exploitation of two-thirds of the world and all who are willing to adjust their present economic and social status so that all might be part of a radical, inclusive, hospitable community. It is necessary for those who are economically stable to remember that to whom much is given, much is expected. Development of these communities will begin with persons who are able to cross economic and social barriers while maintaining respect at a variety of levels. They will be disciples modeling their lives after the Christ who has the ability to transcend gender, race, culture, and class.

These inclusive, hospitable communities will have a creed formulated "We believe" instead of "I believe" because Jesus taught us to pray in community using a prayer that begins "Our . . ." Jesus lived in community. The great majority of the world lives incommunity. The United States is one of the few cultures that believe that society's role is advancement of the individual. The greatest majority of the world believes that the individuals are there to help to advance their particular society communally. Jesus lived in community and calls us to do likewise.

The Lord's Prayer

The Lord's Prayer is one of the firmest foundations of our faith. It was the one prayer Jesus taught us and it is a prayer of community that unites all of us on earth together with all the saints in heaven. It calls for God's Kingdom to come and God's will to be done on earth as it is in heaven. For many of us, this brings visions of all of God's people living in peace and harmony in a world without mental, physical, or emotional borders.

It also teaches us to pray, "Give us this day our daily bread," and indicates that we are aware that our physical, emotional, and spiritual sustenance comes from God. At the same time, it embraces God's economy, which is a creation that has the ability to sustain all of God's creatures. However, that very same creation depends on our embracing God as *our* creator and realizing that in God's economy everyone has enough and those of us with more than enough are called to live simply so that others may simply live.

The Lord's Prayer continues with "Forgive us our trespasses, as we forgive those who trespass against us." In a *Gathering Voices* post on the Thoughtful Christian website, Lara Blackwook Pickrel reflects on seeing a sign on a southwest border:

> The stories shared during our meeting piqued my interest and tugged at my heart, but for some reason what really got me was a single photograph of an official sign on the border. The sign reads: U.S. Property—No Trespassing . . . for some reason I'd never connected "illegal immigration" with trespassing. . . . Finding the language needed to explain myself to Christians who are passionately against undocumented immigrants has always been difficult for me—but now that I've seen that border sign, I think I've found another track, something so basic that all stripes of

Christians know it in their bones: the Lord's Prayer. If, at its core, this immigration debate is about trespassing (as that official border sign asserts) . . . I do hope that each Sunday, as we ask God to "forgive us our trespasses as we forgive those who trespass against us," we all might take a moment to meditate upon the lives of the undocumented immigrants . . . and use our holy imagination to contemplate what such forgiveness could look like if we (and they) were to live it out in the world.[3]

The Lord's Prayer continues with "And lead us not into temptation, but deliver us from evil. For thine is the kingdom and the power and the glory forever. Amen." Perhaps, it simply guides us into praying that we not be tempted to look without regard on any other human being or any part of God's creation. Finally, we affirm that God is God forever and we affirm that belief with an amen. Saying "amen" is saying "So be it!" When we do that, it becomes necessary to take the teachings of Jesus seriously in view of the present day temptation to blame the stranger for the ills of this country. The United States is a predominantly white society that has a history of feeling intellectually, culturally, economically, politically, and religiously superior to the rest of the world. Since the mid-1800s it has embraced the concept of Manifest Destiny, which proposes to make the rest of the world like the United States. After all, it claims to have the highest form of civilization in the world and has obviously accumulated the greatest percentage of the world's wealth.

At this point in history, it appears as though many of its citizens want to keep it that way. In the past, it was acceptable to blame societal ills on the blacks in the land. In recent years, an overt perspective of that type is inappropriate. (The reality is that this is still a very popular covert opinion.) However, many people continue to be in need of a scapegoat to use in explanation of societal ills. Building on false logic and inaccurate and incomplete statistics, some people have found immigrants and refugees to be the perfect targets. If not for "them" all would be well in the land.

Strangers in the Land

Building on the fear of the stranger who looks, acts, and speaks differently, the politicians and media have nurtured xenophobia (fear of the stranger), which has become acceptable on many levels as a new "them" and "us" mentality expands. A picture is often painted of hordes of undocumented immigrants coming into the country through unauthorized border crossings or by being smuggled in on ships or planes. The truth is, according to the U.S. Census Bureau, of the 1.1 million immigrants who arrive in the United States each year, 700,000 enter as documented immigrants, less than 70,000 enter as refugees or persons fleeing persecution, and 485,000 enter as undocumented immigrants.

To get an accurate handle on immigrants, it is important to have some understanding of their roles in society. The United States is not being overrun by immigrants. As of 2010, about 13 percent of the U.S. population was foreign born. By comparison, from 1870 to 1920, the foreign born population made up approximately 15 percent of the population. More than 85 percent of the immigrants come to the United States legally, and about eight out of eleven of them come to join close family members. Most undocumented immigrants don't come to the United States by crossing a border illegally. Six out of ten enter legally with student, tourist, or business visas and become "illegal" when they stay in the United States after their visas expire. In stark contrast to the media image of darker skinned persons illegally entering the country in droves, there is great diversity in the ethnicity of undocumented persons. Many of them come from countries like Canada, England, Ireland, and Poland. Compared to immigrants of color, they are free to live more openly without being questioned about their immigration status.

Undocumented immigrants benefit the U.S. economy. In 2011, the tomato industry in Alabama absorbed massive losses because of a crackdown on undocumented workers, and many growers could not find citizens to harvest the fields. Economist William Ford, from Middle Tennessee State University, has calculated that undocumented immigrants contributed $428 billion to the United States' $13.6 trillion gross domestic product in 2006.[4] Stephen C. Goss, the chief actuary of the Social Security Administration and someone who enjoys bipartisan support for his straightforwardness, said that by 2007, the Social Security trust fund had received a net benefit of somewhere between $120 and $240 billion from unauthorized immigrants. In 2008, the Social Security Administration reported that undocumented immigrants have added eight years of viability to the system. They continue to contribute about $20 billion per year and never receive benefits.[5]

Although it is often claimed that immigrants take American jobs, it is most important to note that millions of American jobs depend on immigrant labor (both documented and undocumented). The Migration Policy Institute reports that by 2030, one-third to one-half of the U.S. labor force will be made up of immigrant workers.[6] In fact, if it were not for immigrant labor, the bottom would fall out of the food and food service industries. Immigrants are willing to take low-paying, backbreaking jobs in harvesting and food preparation that many Americans simply refuse to take. Farms and orchards depend on migrant workers. Meat and poultry slaughtering and packing plants as well as seafood processing plants depend on immigrants to take these undesirable jobs. The movie *A Day Without a Mexican* provides a hypothetical look at what would happen in California should all the "Mexicans" suddenly disappear. The title of the film is an example of the depersonalization of undocumented workers. Although they come from many countries, very often they are simply referred to as "Mexicans" without regard to their true ethnicity. (The film can be rented commercially.)

If all undocumented immigrants were removed from the United States, the negative impact on the country would include $1.757 trillion in annual lost spending, $651.511 billion in annual lost output, and 8.1 million lost jobs.[7]

The unfounded fear of strangers is largely based on love of the almighty dollar and the incorrect perception that undocumented migrants are the cause of economic problems. In reality, rather than take jobs, migrants stimulate the economy and offer opportunities for revitalization of communities. Detroit is an excellent example of immigration benefits.

Latinos and Muslims have been moving to Detroit. Evidence suggests they have been a boon to the city. In 2011 the Immigration Policy Center said that Arab American employment adds $7.7 billion to the economy and $544 million in state taxes; they also support more than 140,000 jobs. Latinos have helped to revitalize Southwest Detroit with $200 million in investments between 1993 and 2000. Rather than taking jobs, immigrants create jobs. Increased populations result in demands for more services and bring more money into the economy and contribute to the tax base.[8]

Immigrants can be a very positive addition to any community. As our communities grow, it is important to build a radical, inclusive, hospitable community of God's people on earth in response to our changing world. That work begins in our homes, churches, and communities. Within the scriptures we can find numerous references to God's mandates to care for the strangers/aliens in the land. We unfortunately live in a place and time in which scriptures have been distorted into a gospel of wealth that ensures that the rich get richer and the poor get poorer.

To properly focus on the scriptural response to immigrants and refugees, the Bible can be embraced as the ultimate immigration handbook. God in the Hebrew Bible and Jesus in the New Testament give specific instructions on how aliens, sojourners, or strangers (immigrants and refugees) are to be treated by God's community on earth. As believers in Jesus the Christ and proponents of the Christian religion, and by studying scriptures, we learn that we are the children of a God who has been actively working with, for, and among the strangers, migrants, immigrants, and refugees of the world since the beginning of history. At times we have all been the stranger, and God has and continues to be with all of us.

When looking at the Bible as the ultimate immigration handbook, we see that it can be used as a guide for developing twenty-first century responses to persons who have been uprooted and are on the move throughout the world. We serve a Christ who knew firsthand what it was to flee for his life, to be hungry, to be scorned, and to be oppressed.

Jesus was very aware of our physical, emotional, and spiritual hunger. In the breaking of the bread at the Last Supper, Jesus, the host, institutes the meal as a sacred time for radical, inclusive hospitality and uses the bread and the wine saying, "This is my body . . . this is my blood." (Matthew 26:26–28), and the Lord's Table becomes the symbol of a table of radical, inclusive hospitality.

The communion table is open to and accessible for all people past, present, and future without regard to their status. When we share the gift of bread and wine within the sacrament of communion, we share it not only with the persons gathered around the table at that moment but with every person who ever has or ever will eat the bread and drink the cup. The table is radically diverse in heaven. We can make it diverse on earth by opening our tables in church and at home to the strangers in our midst.

The Undocumented Jesus

Jesus was not only a refugee and a migrant but was also undocumented as a child in Egypt and at the end of his life. Theologically, we can turn to Hebrews 13:11–16 in reconciling ourselves to the facts of Christ's crucifixion. In it we learn that the bodies of animals whose blood was brought into the sanctuary as a sacrifice for sin were burnt outside the camp. "Therefore, Jesus also suffered outside the city gate in order to sanctify the people by his own blood." The passage also reminded us that we have no lasting city on earth but are looking for the city that is to come. As part of that search, we are to continually offer praise to God and confess God's name. We are then told, "Do not neglect to do good and to share what you have, for such sacrifices are pleasing to God."

As Christians, we believe that Jesus died for the sins of the world, but at that time the theological implications of his death were not considered in handing down his sentence. Jesus was crucified because he was one with the oppressed and marginalized people of that time, and the religious and political powers feared he was instigating an uprising of the poor. The Romans thought Jesus was planning to overthrow those in power. He was one with the stranger, the sojourner, the migrant, the day laborer, the widow, the orphan, the least, the last, and the lost. He did not have the rights of a citizen. Every undocumented migrant in the world can identify with this Jesus. We know that Jesus was crucified "outside the gates" of the city because he was not a Roman citizen. He did not have the required citizenship documents. Crucifixions that took place outside the city gates were reserved for criminals and slaves in the garbage dump of the city. He suffered so others would not have to do the same, and while doing so, he practiced and modeled nonviolence.

The next time you hear of an undocumented person, stop a moment and think of Jesus, cast aside and dying outside of the city.

Remember that we never know when the person we are looking at is Christ among us. We also know that the migrant Christ travels with the migrants. U.S. Border Patrol statistics indicate that between 1998 and 2004, 1,954 people died crossing the U.S–Mexico border, an average of almost one person per day.[9]

Since the passage of the North American Free Trade Agreement (NAFTA), Mexicans have been very negatively impacted. According to a Carnegie Endowment 2006 report,

- Two million Mexicans have been forced out of agriculture. NAFTA has permitted heavily subsidized agricultural products such as corn to be dumped on Mexian markets. Mexican farmers cannot compete with the low prices. There are not other job options for them. They either migrate or starve.
- NAFTA's rules allowed big firms like Walmart to enter the market in Mexico. This put more than 28,000 locally based small manufacturers out of business. (Prices in Mexican Walmarts are comparable to those in the United States.)
- Wages along the border have dropped by 25 percent and typically run sixty cents to one dollar an hour.[10]

As the richest country in the world, the United States must be willing to admit to the role we have played in causing the worldwide migration pattern. As we study scripture, we learn that during Christ's time on earth, he was a refugee, an asylum seeker, a migrant, and undocumented. He also reached out to the other and crossed physical, emotional, mental, economic, gender, and educational borders. He is a model for the United Methodist open hearts, open doors, and open minds policy. Christ is in us, the Holy Spirit is with us, and God taught us how to care for the strangers among us. In Matthew 4:19 Jesus said to the men who became his disciples, "Follow me, and I will make you fish for people." He is saying that very same thing to each of us. It is up to us to decide our next steps. We make those decisions knowing that by offering lives of service and sacrifice we will be following in Christ's footsteps and holding onto his hand with each and every step forward while reaching out to the other and the other and the other throughout eternity.

Notes

1. Mother Teresa, quoted in Eileen Egan, "Dorothy Day, Pilgrim of Peace," in *A Revolution of the Heart: Essays on the Catholic Worker,* ed. Patrick G. Coy (Philadelphia: Temple University Press, 1988), 105.
2. Personal communication with Bill Mefford.
3. Lara Blackwook Pickrel, "Forgive Us Our Trespasses," *Gathering Voices,* March 11, 2011, http://blog.thethoughtfulchristian.com/2011/03/forgive-us-our-trespasses.html.
4. Travis Loller, "Many Illegal Immigrants Pay Up at Tax Time," *USA Today,* April 4, 2008.
5. Ibid.
6. B. Lindsey Lowell, Julia Gelatt, and Jeanne Batalova, *Immigrants and Labor Force Trends: The Future, Past, and Present* (Washington, DC: Migration Policy Institute, 2006), 1.
7. The Perryman Group, *An Essential Resource: An Analysis of the Economic Impact of Undocumented Workers on Business Activity in the U.S. with Estimated Effects by State and by Industry* (Houston, TX: Americans for Immigration Reform, 2008), http://americansforimmigrationreform.com/files/Impact_of_the_Undocumented_Workforce.pdf.
8. Immigration Policy Center, "New Americans in the Great Lakes State," July 4, 2009, www.immigrationpolicy.org/just-facts/new-americans-great-lakes-state.
9. "National Briefing, Southwest: New Mexico: A Mass for Border Crossers," *New York Times,* November 3, 2004, http://query.nytimes.com/gst/fullpage.html?res=9C05E4DB163CF930A35752C1A9629C8B63.
10. Roger Bybee and Carolyn Winter, "Immigration Flood Unleashed by NAFTA's Disastrous Impact on Mexican Economy," April 25, 2006, www.commondreams.org/views06/0425-30.htm.

Chapter 7
Embracing Radical Hospitality

Do not neglect to show hospitality to strangers,
for by doing that, some have entertained
angels without knowing it.
Remember those who are in prison,
as though you were in prison with them;
those who are being tortured, as though you
yourselves were being tortured.

—Hebrews 13:2–3

Hospitality is a foundation of the Christian faith. We pride ourselves on hospitality committees, church events, and personal gifts of hospitality in our churches and homes. We care for our members, families, and friends in generous, kind, and loving ways. This basic understanding of hospitality, which has been culturally and theologically developed, is the foundation on which we can develop radical hospitality and reinstate the biblical concept of hospitality in our lives and churches. It is based in offering hospitality to the stranger, the sojourner, the alien, the migrant, and the foreigner by following the biblical word of God. We are to follow that word because "once we were strangers in this land." The United States is a nation of immigrants, and, unless we are 100 percent Native American, we can all trace our immigration history to another land.

Deuteronomy 6:10–12 reminds us to remember God in our response to being in this land as a result of our migration or that of our ancestors:

> When the Lord your God has brought you into the land
> that he swore to your ancestors, to Abraham, to Isaac,
> and to Jacob, to give you—a land with fine, large cities
> that you did not build, houses filled with all sorts of goods
> that you did not fill, hewn cisterns that you did not hew,
> vineyards and olive groves that you did not plant—and
> when you have eaten your fill, take care that you do not
> forget the Lord, who brought you out of the land of Egypt,
> out of the house of slavery.

This and other Deuteronomy passages stress the importance of being one with strangers in the land. It also stresses being careful to not forget the Lord who brought us here and out of slavery. We are to live with thankful hearts, remembering that life can change in an instant. We are called to respond by being the hands and hearts of Christ to all we meet.

Judith Pierre-Okerson, board member of the Women's Division of the General Board of Global Ministries, the policymaking body of United Methodist Women, has lived out the scriptural call to be the hands and hearts of Christ to all we meet. In the 1980s she and other members of her family were government employees in Haiti. Ms. Pierre-Okerson was not home at the time of a coup that removed the president of Haiti from office, but her mother and two brothers were. A neighbor risked his own security to come knock on the back door and tell them a gang was at the front gate. They had to run for their lives. When they returned home, nothing was left. Their home had been destroyed and looted. All that remained was the clothes they were wearing. In an instant their lives changed.

The family rebuilt their lives, and Ms. Pierre-Okerson eventually emigrated to the United States and has blessed many of us with her teachings, her words, her actions, her theology, and her willingness to give radical inclusive hospitality to strangers in the land. She shared with me how blessed she feels that God was with her and her family and helped them move past the unfortunate experience and rebuild their lives in a very short time.

Church culture and practice often seeks the best for members and persons close to the church. Biblical hospitality requires taking care of the strangers, especially the widows, the orphans, and the strangers as seen in Deuteronomy 14:28–29:

> Every third year you shall bring out the full tithe of your produce for that year, and store it within your towns; the Levites, because they have no allotment or inheritance with you, as well as the resident aliens, the orphans, and the widows in your towns, may come and eat their fill so that the Lord your God may bless you in all the work that you undertake.

Isaiah 58:6–10 (which we saw in Chapter 5) also addresses the importance of seeking justice and caring for those with needs. Isaiah was voicing a response to the cry of God's people who asked why, although they were fasting, God was not answering prayers as they desired. The prophet delivered God's response, which reads in part:

> Is not this the fast that I choose: to loose the bonds of injustice, to undo the thongs of the yoke, to let the oppressed go free, and to break every yoke? Is it not to share your bread with the hungry, and bring the homeless poor into your house; when you see the naked, to cover them, and not to hide yourself from your own kin? . . . If you

offer your food to the hungry and satisfy the needs of the afflicted, then your light shall rise in the darkness and your gloom be like the noonday.

This passage reminds us that God calls on us to care for those in need and is a precursor to Matthew 25:31–46, which is Jesus' strongest statement on how we obtain eternal life. The passage effectively states that we are to be in service to the people of God who are in need if we desire to enter into eternal life. Although this is a very well known passage, it is very often neglected in discussions of how one enters the kin-dom of heaven.

When the Son of Man comes in his glory, and all the angels with him, then he will sit on the throne of his glory. All the nations will be gathered before him, and he will separate people one from another as a shepherd separates the sheep from the goats, and he will put the sheep at his right hand and the goats at the left. Then the king will say to those at his right hand, "Come, you that are blessed by my Father, inherit the kingdom prepared for you from the foundation of the world; for I was hungry and you gave me food, I was thirsty and you gave me something to drink, I was a stranger and you welcomed me, I was naked and you gave me clothing, I was sick and you took care of me, I was in prison and you visited me." Then the righteous will answer him, "Lord, when was it that we saw you hungry and gave you food, or thirsty and gave you something to drink? And when was it that we saw you a stranger and welcomed you, or naked and gave you clothing? And when was it that we saw you sick or in prison and visited you?" And the king will answer them, "Truly I tell you, just as you did it to one of the least of these who are members of my family, you did it to me." Then he will say to those at his left hand, "You that are accursed, depart from me into the eternal fire prepared for the devil and his angels; for I was hungry and you gave me no food, I was thirsty and you gave me nothing to drink, I was a stranger and you did not welcome me, naked and you did not give me clothing, sick and in prison and you did not visit me." Then they also will answer, "Lord, when was it that we saw you hungry or thirsty or a stranger or naked or sick or in prison, and did not take care of you?" Then he will answer them, "Truly I tell you, just as you did not do it to one of the least of these, you did not do it to me." And these will go away into eternal punishment, but the righteous into eternal life.

Jesus explained that to inherit eternal life, we must feed the hungry, give drink to the thirsty, welcome the stranger, clothe the naked, and visit the sick and imprisoned. It is simple—do so and earn eternal life. Neglect to do so and earn eternal punishment. Practicing radical, inclusive hospitality enables us to respond to all of Christ's requests and to be the hands and feet of Christ in the world.

This passage demonstrates that there are many opportunities to follow and serve Christ. For example, when we help an undocumented immigrant or family, we serve in most if not all of the ways Jesus asks us to serve. They travel to this country in need of food, drink, clothing, shelter, and, most important, a new life and employment. They desperately need radical, inclusive hospitality.

In 2001, Ypsilanti First United Methodist Church in Ypsilanti, Michigan, made a conscious decision to open its doors to the neighborhood and its many immigrants. They first started English as a second language classes. In 2002 they started small group faith communities. In 2004 they started a Spanish worship service. The Rev. Melanie Carey, who was the pastor of the church at that time said, "We are one church with two languages, and three times a year we have bilingual worship services all together."

In 2005, one of the church families faced voluntary deportation back to Mexico. This was their first exposure to the U.S. immigration system. In 2006 a member was deported, leaving her U.S. citizen husband and young children behind. In 2008 a member of the board of trustees was detained and deported, leaving his daughter and wife behind. Then Jasmine came into their lives.

At seventeen years of age, Jasmine, a U.S. citizen, saw her undocumented Guatemalan mother arrested, detained, and deported. Jasmine was not given a chance to kiss or hug her mother or say good-bye. After her mother was deported, her father, who was undocumented and feared deportation, returned to Guatemala with her twelve-year-old sister. Jasmine stayed in Michigan to finish her education, caring for herself, the family trailer, and the family dog. In addition to going to school, Jasmine had to work to pay the rent and other family bills.

It was not an easy struggle. Jasmine was alone, often hungry, and with no real support system. Jasmine writes, "I heard about this wonderful person, Melanie Carey, pastor at First United Methodist Church. . . . She supported me in any way possible. The church helped me financially in driving to school and many other things. When the congregation heard about my frequent weekends going without food, a group set up a weekly rotation to provide groceries. When I ultimately lost the cleaning job, a member found me a clerical position."

Ms. Carey's family became Jasmine's family. They had been thinking of hosting an exchange student and realized that "perhaps Jasmine was the exchange student God had in mind for us

. . . only she wasn't from another country as she is a U.S. citizen, born in Chicago."

The congregation was distressed by an immigration system that would break up a family and leave a teenager alone to raise herself. They wrote advocacy letters and became involved with Justice for Our Neighbors (JFON) to help others in similar situations. Unfortunately, there are thousands and thousands of Jasmines, and the number is growing each day. *Story from "Jasmine's Story" by Jasmine Franco for the General Board of Church and Society, August 6, 2010 (www.umc-gbcs.org). Supplemented with personal communication from Melanie Carey. Jasmine's story, in her words, can be found in the appendix of the participant's guide (included at the end of this book).*

Immigration Detention

Immigrants and asylum seekers who are detained in the United States are in need of a caring and loving person to let them know that they are not alone. Radical, inclusive, hospitable communities can visit them to let them know that there are followers of Christ seeking to welcome them and provide a place for them in their community should they be released from prison. Across the country, United Methodist Women members are offering hope and friendship to immigration detainees by visiting them and advocating for justice.

The U.S. government detains more than 440,000 men, women, and children per year. This is more than triple the number of people in detention ten years ago. They are in close to three hundred facilities at an annual cost of more than $1.7 billion. This includes government owned and operated services processing centers, privately owned contract facilities, and many local jails holding contracts for detaining immigrants on a per diem basis.[1]

Being in violation of an immigration law is not a crime. It is a civil violation for which immigrants go through a process to see whether they have a right to stay in the United States. Immigrants detained are in noncriminal custody and are called "detainees" rather than "inmates." Persons detained include undocumented migrants who have committed no crime, immigrants who came legally and overstayed, victims of trafficking, asylum seekers, and immigrants with a past criminal record who have already completed their sentences. If they were citizens they would have been released. However, after completing their sentences, immigrants are moved to a detention center for deportation proceedings.

Detention can be a traumatizing and humiliating event for persons who have never broken a law and find themselves behind bars. In addition, with the passage of the Illegal Immigration Reform and Immigrant Responsibility Act of 1996, any immigrant (including green card holders) who is questioned by the police and found to have committed a crime punishable by a year in jail (even if he or she were never jailed) is considered an aggravated felon and can be detained for deportation. It is common for an upstanding U.S. resident with a job, home, and American family to be detained and deported because of a run-in with the law that took place years ago. In addition, torture survivors, victims of trafficking, and other vulnerable groups can be detained for months or even years, further aggravating their isolation, depression, and other mental health problems associated with their trauma.

United Methodist Women has identified the detention of immigrants as a key area of concern and advocacy. They are especially concerned about women and children in detention. Between 1998 and 2007 the United States removed 108,434 immigrants who were parents of U.S. citizen children.[2] United Methodist Women has partnered with the Detention Watch Network (www.detention-watchnetwork.org) to encourage visitation in detention centers. This ministry is developed in the Wesleyan tradition of prison visitation as well as of following Christ's mandate to visit the prisoners. John Wesley believed that faithful Christian discipleship required visiting those in the prisons as an expression of love for God and love for neighbor. Wesley regularly visited because there he experienced God's grace and saw the image of God. The experience of visiting detainees will also help other United Methodists and people of faith understand the plight of and advocate for improved treatment of all immigrants.

In 2008, United Methodist Women in New York City became leaders in a series of immigration detention center vigils by demonstrating in front of the Varick Street Detention Center in Manhattan. Other United Methodist Women groups across the country have followed suit in mounting demonstrations to express their concern over injustices in immigration detention. Across the country, United Methodist Women advocates continue to work with a broad coalition for an end to the detention of many detainees. These include families, survivors of torture, and victims of trafficking, asylum seekers, and other vulnerable groups, including pregnant women, children, and seriously ill individuals.

Texas has a very high concentration of immigration detention centers. More than 10,000 immigrants may be detained there at any time because they do not have proper documents. The Rio Grande Valley, a Detainee Visitation Project (RGDVP) offers friendship, support, and companionship to immigration detainees. The trained visitors are matched with detainees and commit to visiting detainees at least twice a month.

The RGDVP works in conjunction with a national network of visitation projects including the Detention Visitation Network, La Frontera Ministries, and United Methodist Women. RGDVP visitors "seek to provide a compassionate face and an affirmation of humanity . . . not visiting as social workers or lawyers, but simply as friends." The visitors are the face of Christ and a ray of hope for detainees alone in this strange land.

Deaconess Cindy Johnson, former United Methodist Women immigration intern, coordinated advocacy and visitation for detainees in 2011 and states, "There are other just and humane ways of dealing with brothers and sisters who migrate/immigrate because they need to. The detention of immigrants is the fastest growing prison industry in the United States because it profits private industry at the expense of men, women, and children—families seeking to survive and earn their daily bread."

She is especially concerned about women crossing the border. She has developed a special relationship with some of the women who cross the border, members of the border patrol, and staff members in area housing shelters. When a particularly vulnerable pregnant woman is picked up, it is not unusual for the border patrol to bring her to a local shelter. Cindy meets the women and with other volunteers offers them hands of friendship, sees them through delivery, and helps them navigate the complexities of U.S. immigration law.

This practice of radical hospitality stores up treasures in heaven and provides innumerable joys here on earth for both the disciples and the strangers who are recipients of loving, radical, inclusive hospitality. The best known New Testament passage is Hebrews 13:2–3, "Do not neglect to show hospitality to strangers, for by doing that, some have entertained angels without knowing it. Remember those who are in prison, as though you were in prison with them; those who are being tortured, as though you yourselves were being tortured."

Echo Park, California, sits snugly between Los Angeles and Hollywood. It is a combination of struggling families and creative Hollywood people. Echo Park United Methodist Church was once predominantly Anglo, but immigrants were always welcome and integral to the church. Thirty years ago they came from the Philippines, other countries in Asia, then the Caribbean, and now Central America. The majority of church members are from immigrant families. The congregation embraced the sanctuary movement of the 1980s, which saw Central Americans fleeing persecution and seeking asylum. It is a United Methodist Welcoming Congregation, open to all immigrants and part of the New Sanctuary Movement, whose members speak out against the separation of families due to unjust immigration laws and inject the voice of faith into the immigration dialogue. Pastor David Farley says, "We've called this growing network of faith communities the New Sanctuary Movement. But in reality it's an ancient movement, as old as Abraham and Sarah welcoming three strangers and entertaining angels unawares, as old as the embrace of Ruth and Naomi, as old as the radical hospitality of the New Testament Church, as old as the Underground Railroad."

Echo Park United Methodist Church works with other churches and the California-Pacific Immigration Task Force in establishing legal clinics, offering radical hospitality, serving the community through outreach programs, and hosting art, spirituality, and social justice gatherings. It helps with struggles on worker issues and domestic workers rights. The congregation, which includes an active, diverse United Methodist Women ministry, is involved in ministry in most areas that touch the marginalized.

In 2011 the church hosted the first "Immigration 101" clinic for clergy, staff, and lay leaders to provide basic knowledge with which to answer immigration questions. Through an educational clinic developed by the United Methodist Immigration Task Force's "DREAM Summer Intern" (an undocumented law student), Echo Park United Methodist Church is helping to provide church leaders some basic answers and references about the realities immigrants face and the services available to them.

In September 2011 Stephanie Kimec, a US-2 young adult missionary, was assigned to Echo Park by the Immigration Task Force. With the support of the congregation she will work on expanding neighborhood immigration clinics and organizing a network of immigrant welcoming congregations.

When asked for advice to congregations seeking to start or expand immigration ministries, Mr. Farley replied, "I think the best first steps are children and family related programs because the immigrant population will do anything for its children. That's how we became involved. There is also connecting with organizations or groups working with immigrant communities and asking how the church might be of service. Reaching the people through family-related programs and just being aware of every opportunity to build relationships." *From personal communication with Naomi Madsen and David Farley, Echo Park United Methodist Church, Echo Park, California.*

This scripture stresses that disciples are to identify with and work to help strangers in all circumstances, especially in very troubling situations. Migrant workers, many undocumented, are in need of welcome centers in the churches where they can receive food, showers, fresh clothing, and help in orienting themselves to the area and in finding safety and sanctuary. New immigrants also often need help in adjusting to a lifestyle that is most often very different from the culture of their country of origin.

Jesus was very clear about the importance of putting others first. All four gospels record his having said, "Those whoever find their life will lose it, and those who lose their life for my sake will find it" (Matthew 10:39). To follow Christ means to model one's life after his life. To follow means to actively live a life of radical, inclusive love and to be in ministry to strangers in need. It also teaches us to accept and to love the strangers in our midst, even though they may be considered by others as neither respectable nor valuable. In Matthew 22:36-39, when asked which commandment was the greatest, Jesus replied, "'You shall love the Lord your God with all your heart, and with all your soul, and with all your mind.' This is the greatest and first commandment. And a second is like it: 'You shall love your neighbor as yourself.'" John Chrysostom (a fourth century saint) insisted that Christian hospitality was to welcome not persons of high status but to deliberately welcome those who brought little into the encounter. "Hospitality was a significant context for transcending status boundaries . . . in fact, to entertain persons who had few needs was not really hospitality at all."[3]

Jesus welcomed the outcasts of society, Samaritans and other foreigners, including a woman with seven demons and a despised tax collector. The religious establishment did not. These are the people who are not welcomed into many religious institutions today. They were the people whom St. Jerome challenged the early clergy to welcome. Christ was then and is now the stranger knocking at our doors.

Recently I preached in a large church with a very small and aging congregation located in a very diverse part of a city. An after-worship coffee hour was listed in the bulletin. I went to the coffee pot and was joined by a homeless man and an immigrant grandmother seeking prayers for a granddaughter. No one else joined us or greeted us. I could not help but wonder whether they had missed meeting the Christ among us. However, it is important to add, members of this congregation have told me they want to welcome newcomers; they simply have no idea how to talk to strangers.

To develop a ministry of radical hospitality, the members of the church must respond to Christ's call, "Follow me," and love as Christ loved and reach out to others as Christ reached out to us.

1 Corinthians 13:1–13 guides us in developing Christ-like love in all areas of our lives. In seeking to develop radical, inclusive hospitality in all relationships, we can test ourselves by reading the passage and using our name in place of the words "love" and "it" wherever they appear in verses four to eight:

> Love is patient; love is kind; love is not envious or boastful or arrogant or rude. It does not insist on its own way; it is not irritable or resentful; it does not rejoice in wrongdoing, but rejoices in the truth. It bears all things, believes all things, hopes all things, endures all things. Love never ends.

As we ponder this passage, we can't help but consider our country's responses to immigrants. Are we open and loving or irritable and resentful? Are we willing to expand our circle and invite strangers in and move out to risk being the stranger who receives rather than offers radical, inclusive hospitality? Christ taught us to love and modeled a life of being open to an ever-enlarging circle of people who were strangers on the way to becoming friends and family. It also means being willing to give our time and talents in service to others.

It is possible that some of us are being called to leave our comfortable church to join a completely different congregation to learn to receive as the other rather than give to the other. It is one thing to open our churches to all; it is quite another to learn what it is like to be the other and enter into ministry as the outsider with immigrants, refugees, asylum seekers, and migrants. Across the country many churches embrace one particular group or another: Korean, Chinese, Hispanic, Indonesian, African, Polish, Irish, German, and others. Some think of these churches as ethnic churches, and many are, but many are also very open to welcome the other.

In the same way, some churches focus on a particular geographic, ethnic, economic, or social area. They have congregations who are comfortable with who they are and are willing to be open to having the "other" join their congregation. With very few exceptions, United Methodist churches are open to welcoming the other. Unfortunately, some churches would rather close their doors than embrace change and welcome strangers into their circle of local church family hospitality and love. Some churches are also actively involved in seeking to remove all undocumented persons, even though the undocumented of this land have direct ties to at least fifty million American families.

Churches with open hearts, open minds, and open doors are seeing diverse congregations developing to match the demographics of their areas. However, other churches are still struggling to cross those boundaries and become one with the other. It is not easy to cross an unknown boundary. We are the strangers the churches of the others are waiting to welcome. Are we willing to be the first to cross the boundaries?

When I pastored a small church in Pennsylvania, a young black man entered the church and stood in the narthex on several occasions but always left before the service ended. I was the only one who saw him because of the pulpit vantage point. He returned very early on a Palm Sunday to ask if he could worship with us. After being assured of his welcome, he explained that four area churches had suggested that he find another, more comfortable place to worship. In truth, the congregants were white. As we move forward in building God's community, we need to remember that across the world there are Christians and members of other faiths who will not accept perceived outsiders.

As we seek to welcome newcomers, with or without documents, let's ask ourselves, how would we feel walking in to a church on Sunday morning where we don't know the language, don't know the worship traditions, and don't look like anyone else? To learn the answer, find just such a church in your area and visit, not once but repeatedly. You might find blessings beyond measure through hospitality to the stranger offered to you as the stranger.

The following are responses to the mandate to offer hospitality to the stranger: Food to immigrants here and abroad; water to the migrants crossing the desert; an open church door to the stranger with nowhere to turn; clothing to the newly arrived migrant or refugee; medical care for migrant workers, immigrants, refugees, and asylum seekers; and prison visits to detained asylum seekers and immigrants. Responding to their needs can be the foundation of a ministry to the strangers in our communities and are opportunities to practice radical, inclusive hospitality.

People working with immigrants, migrants, refugees, and asylum seekers are often heard wondering how to convince more churchgoers to help them. Jesus was very clear in his message: Help the stranger, the prisoner, the homeless, the hungry, the thirsty, and the naked and earn eternal life. Don't help them and earn eternal punishment.

John Wesley voiced this idea slightly differently. He was asked what good it did to feed and clothe people's bodies when they might be going to hell. He responded, "Whether they will finally be lost or saved, you are expressly commanded to feed the hungry and clothe the naked. If you can, and do not, whatever becomes of them, you shall go into everlasting fire."[4]

Our response to the other is directly related to our response to God. Radical, inclusive hospitality is not an optional practice. According to seminary professor Christine D. Pohl,

> It is, instead, a necessary practice in the community of faith. One of the key Greek words for hospitality, *philoxenia*, combines the general word for love or affection for people who are connected by kinship or faith (*phileo*), and the word for stranger (*xenos*). Thus, etymologically and practically, in the New Testament, hospitality is closely connected to love. Because *philoxenia* includes the word for stranger, hospitality's orientation towards strangers is also more apparent in Greek than in English.[5]

The mandate remains clear. We are to live lives of radical, inclusive hospitality, to recognize that Christ comes to us in the form of the stranger, and to be one with the prisoners, the persecuted, the undocumented, the refugee, the migrant, the immigrant, the stranger. Throughout the Bible we see people moving and witness new life as lives are changed through contact with Christ and his disciples. Paul reinforces this teaching in Romans 12:13, with, "Contribute to the needs of the saints; extend hospitality to strangers."

Jesus' last message to his disciples was a migration message. It is a statement that not only calls for migration but insists on it. Matthew 28:18–20 is the great commission, in which Jesus says, "All authority in heaven and on earth has been given to me. Go therefore and make disciples of all nations, baptizing them in the name of the Father and of the Son and of the Holy Spirit, and teaching them to obey everything that I have commanded you. . . . And remember I am with you always, to the end of the age."

Jesus assumed the role of the migrant Jesus traveling with every disciple moving throughout the world. Remember that at that time,

North America was not a known part of the world. It would have been considered the ends of the earth. The question is, are we obeying Jesus? Yet the story was not over at that point. On the day of Pentecost, as promised in John 16:13–15, Christ sent the Holy Spirit to guide us into all the truth:

> When the Spirit of truth comes, he will guide you into all the truth; for he will not speak on his own, but will speak whatever he hears, and he will declare to you the things that are to come. He will glorify me, because he will take what is mine and declare it to you. All that the Father has is mine. For this reason I said that he will take what is mine and declare it to you.

The Book of Acts

In Acts 2, a rush of violent wind brought divided tongues of fire and rested on each of them, and "all of them were all filled with the Holy Spirit and began to speak in other languages, as the Spirit gave them ability." The crowd, a microcosm of the then known world, were amazed. Each heard the disciples speaking in their native languages about God's deeds of power.

Those who heard in their own languages were visitors from and residents of most of the then known world: Asia, Africa, Europe, and the Middle East. On hearing God's word, about three thousand were baptized and became part of the fledgling Jewish community that would first be known as the People of the Way and later become known as Christians, first in Antioch (Acts 11:26) and then elsewhere as the term spread.

We also see the institution of a Christian sacrament in which the Baptism that took place and continues to this day as a sign of belonging to the body of Christ. In addition, as members of the new community, the disciples "devoted themselves to the apostles' teaching and fellowship, to the breaking of bread and the prayers" (Acts 2:42).

Members of the new community of believers became migrant messengers, taking Christ's teachings throughout the known world. According to tradition, traveling with them was Mary Magdalene who was the first to see the risen Christ and who is referred to by the Orthodox Church as the apostle to the apostles. She traveled to Rome and other parts of Italy to preach. She was there with Paul and at a very old age migrated to Ephesus, where she worked with the apostle John. Mary was not the only female disciple, other women, who were equals in Christ's community, were among those sent to tell the good news.

Christ's followers recognized that divisions among all of humankind had been dismantled. Galatians 3:28 states, "There is no longer Jew or Greek, there is no longer slave or free; there is no longer male and female; for all of you are one in Christ Jesus." This is followed by Galatians 5:14: "For the whole law is summed up in a single commandment, 'You shall love your neighbor as yourself.'" They took this message with them and they traveled as immigrants and migrants. They were and are imprisoned; they were and are persecuted and exiled.

Religious persecution continues to this day and is internationally recognized as grounds for asylum. John Calvin believed that "no duty can be more pleasing or acceptable to God" than offering hospitality to religious refugees. This he believed was a sacred form of hospitality.[6]

The early disciples believed they were strangers in this life moving on to the heavenly kingdom. In 1 Peter 2:11–13, they are reminded that they are aliens and exiles in this world. They are the beginning of a long line of pilgrim people and a part of the continuing biblical migratory cycle following the mandates of God, the teachings of

Christ, and the guidance of the Holy Spirit. The New Testament ends with John's writing of the Book of Revelation, in exile, on the Isle of Patmos. The biblical story that began with migration ends with migration and exile. It continues to this day as the migrant God accompanies each and every one on his or her journey of hope. It extends far into the future, with the New Jerusalem coming from heaven to earth. When that happens, the circle of migration will be completed and the world made new.

Those of us living in the present "end times" have cause for concerns as the U.S. Congress and state and local governments develop programs that target immigrants for exclusion and deportation. The reversal of this trend will call for a coming together of very diverse people filled with the desire to have God's community come to earth in such a manner that the lion will lie down with the lamb and churches will be open to all of God's people. In order for this to happen, the love for one another must be undergirded by justice. Martin Luther King Jr. was very explicit about the principles of love and justice. In fact, he made the principle of love secondary to justice: "It is not enough to talk about love. Love is one of the principal parts of the Christian faith. There is another side called justice. . . . Justice is love correcting that which would work against love." Standing beside love is always justice."[7]

Living in a Welcoming Community

Mr. King believed that the dignity and worth of every person must be recognized, respected, and validated. He was articulating a universal dream that was "grounded in eternity and not given by people."[8] Until we are all free to be exactly the person God has created us to be, none of us are free. As long as there is one person who cannot walk the streets with his or her head held high and feel the sunshine on his or her face, none of us can truly walk with our heads held high.

Diverse groups of people working together—not in groups of *them* or *us*—are the starting point for a new theology of hospitality that crosses cultural and racial boundaries. It seeks to welcome all peoples into a community that by its very diversity speaks of the radical inclusiveness and communal model of the Holy Trinity.

It will involve groups who accept Jesus as the supreme universal disclosure of the word of God for all. It is a calling of the masses to radical inclusive discipleship. This theology is one that calls us to be mindful of theologian Dietrich Bonheoffer's statement that "when Christ calls a man, he bids him to come and die." Just as Christ came and died for us, he bids us to come and die for the stranger (the immigrant, the migrant, and the refugee). "Discipleship is submission to the law of Christ which is the law of the cross."[9]

In following Jesus, by carrying the cross of the stranger we must be ready for the rejection that it entails. But we must also recognize that those who will reject us, when we become the voice of the marginalized, are often the very people who will eventually join us if we persevere. If we do not persevere, we will one day have to answer to Christ. If we persevere, we follow Christ's words in John 8:31b–32, "If you continue in my word, you are truly my disciples; you will know the truth, and the truth will make you free." By following God's word, we are set free. In following that word we discover that it will also set the marginalized of our land free and free us to live ever more fulfilling lives through embracing radical, inclusive hospitality that dismantles barriers between and among people.

We begin to live in complete freedom by embracing Christ's commandments with our hearts, souls, and minds. We obey the word of Christ and love the Lord our God above all things and all people. We love our neighbors as ourselves. Following Jesus, we go one step further and practice his command to love our enemies. Disciples who practice radical, inclusive hospitality live by a simple creed of love with open hearts, open minds, and open doors. They see Christ's unjust suffering and exclusion from the inner religious circles of his day pointing to the overwhelming presence of Christ with those in our world who are suffering as victims of the god of mammon's followers who refuse to welcome and embrace all of God's people. As radical, hospitable disciples and theologians we see the immigrants, migrants, and refugees all over the world as modern day Christ's crucified and consecrate our lives to work to stop the crucifixions. We seek to become servants and peacemakers, bringing the light and life of Jesus Christ to resurrect a dying world. We seek to build a radical, inclusive, hospitable, universal community that embraces all of humankind. A community based on proclamation, servanthood, and community and focused on our neighbors, world, and God rather than on ourselves.

Living in community, we live in the power of the Spirit and are transformed into the likeness of Christ. This happens through God's grace. It begins with justification, continues in sanctification, and moves on toward vocation, which leads to perfection in loving as God loves. This vocational call to community is the fruit of justification and sanctification. It is leaving the church community, while remaining a part of the church community, to go into the world and work and get our hands dirty. It is taking to heart Hebrews 13:2–3, "Do not neglect to show hospitality to strangers, for by doing that some have entertained angels without knowing it. Remember those who are in prison as though you were in prison with them; those who are being tortured as though you yourselves were being tortured." It is to remember the Sermon on the Mount and Matthew 25:31–46 and to remember that our transition from God's community on earth to God's community in heaven will involve our hearing Jesus say, "As you did it to the least of these, you did it to me."

The Sacraments

For Christians, participation in God's community includes participation in God's sacraments of baptism and communion. Baptism is the sacrament of "God's solidarity with the world . . . human solidarity in Christ with each other . . . and human solidarity with the whole groaning creation."[10] Communion is the sacrament of the "sharing of the divine life with humanity . . . human participation in the divine life by sharing life with each other . . . the shared life and common destiny of humanity and nature."[11]

Baptism breaks down all boundaries between peoples. It brings unity to diversity through the action of the God who shows no partiality (Acts 10:34). It gives recipients a new identity as children of the triune God. It is a sacrament of human solidarity in Christ and with one another and with respect for our cultures, traditions, and worship practices. The newly baptized, the Christ, and the congregation make up a new community. It is a call to have us, as members of the family of God, uplift and welcome all of God's people and creation. Our salvation is tied to the salvation of the stranger, the world, and God who is in all relationships. We cannot get to heaven alone; rather, we travel with one hand in front of us holding Christ's hand and the other hand behind us, bringing others with us: "Hospitality makes room even for the one who is frighteningly different. . . . Hospitality treats people respectfully, as if they are sacred, because they are sacred, because they are. Even the other, the stranger, the one who is nothing at all like me. He brings the Divine to me, too."[12]

The communion of saints is a universal time event in which past, present, and future, along with heaven and earth, become simply the Now. The communion table epitomizes the remembrance of Christ's sacrifice. When we share the body and blood of Jesus Christ, we truly embrace the reality that there is only one race—the human race—and we become a new, more highly defined part of the human race in Christ Jesus. We are new community that has all colors and social standings and the blood of Jesus flowing through our veins. Jesus said, "This is my blood of the covenant, which is poured out for many" (Mark 14:24). Participation in communion makes us all blood relatives and a new people guided by the Holy Spirit. This new blood intermingled with our old blood is the creation of a new humanity. The table fellowship of the ancient church had commonalities that are shared in contemporary radical, inclusive, hospitable communities.

Christine D. Pohl states in *Making Room: Recovering Hospitality as a Christian Tradition:*

> The practice of hospitality almost always includes eating meals together. Sustained hospitality requires a light hold on material possessions and a commitment to a simplified lifestyle. The most potent setting for hospitality is in the overlap of private and public space; hospitality flourishes at the intersection of the personal, intimate characteristics of the home and the transforming expectations of the church. Practitioners view hospitality as a sacred practice and find God is specially present in guest/host relationships. There is a mutual blessing in hospitality; practitioners consistently comment that they receive more than they give. Almost all insist that the demands of hospitality can only be met by persons sustained by a strong life of prayer and times of solitude.[13]

In working toward the new humanity, we must remember that Christ died for *all* people. Christ did not die for only one people, one group, or one religion. Christ was very obvious in reaching out to the other/the stranger, in crossing over to the other, in making it very clear that everyone had worth and value. Christ lived in tension among a number of communities, holding them together as the center of communities that model the relationship of a three-part community. In acknowledgement of this, it is important to recognize that along with the concepts of various Christian communities, there is a larger community on earth that is the Christian community and the non-Christian community, which, when viewed through the eyes of the followers of Jesus, are brought together as an inclusive triune community with Christ as its center. Christ set up this community for us when he repeatedly included the stranger in his life. He further solidified it when he reached out and told the thief, "Today you will be with me in Paradise" (Luke 23:43). As followers of Christ, we are to remember that we can only perfect a triune community when we truly understand that God's community is the whole world. We take life seriously when we embrace radical, inclusive hospitality and celebrate the sanctity of life.

By our best and worst attempts at hospitality we say to ourselves and the world: You are not alone. We need each other.[14] When this happens, we give life and hope to the neediest among us. We must remember and answer with our lives in a way that will bring life everlasting to all.

"Hospitality becomes for the Christian community a way of being the sacrament of God's love in the world."[15] As we work to form that radical, inclusive, hospitable community, as we wait for walls to come down, as we wait for God's love to be held in the heart of every human being, we must hold on to the vision of the perfect community in which the heart, hands, and Spirit of God in the heavenly community reach down to the lifted hands, hearts, and spirits of the earthly community and form a circle of love without barriers.

This is the vision of the radical, creative, hospitable, inclusive theologian. It is our job to "write the vision; make it plain on the tablets, so that a runner may read it. For there is still a vision for the appointed time; it speaks of the end, and does not lie. If it seems to tarry, wait for it; it will surely come, it will not delay" (Habakkuk 2:2–3).

The vision will be realized when we all truly learn to love, welcome, and accept one another. It will come together when we build and become radical, hospitable communities open to the stranger God who stands outside and knocks.

Our faith connects us with all the saints that have gone on before. In 2004, interfaith groups held a border pilgrimage to pray for our undocumented sisters and brothers and to visit the graves of hundreds of them buried in the Holtville, California, cemetery. It was a most compelling visit, as we searched for their section of graves and discovered hundreds of small white crosses, some with teddy bears next to them to signify the graves of unknown children. That evening we held a worship service and as part of that service read the names of dozens of persons who had died on their trip north. The next day one among us decided to share what she had experienced during the worship service. It was an experience we had all had but had been holding close to our hearts and in our spirits.

As the names were called, we took turns answering "Presente" to indicate that all who had died were with us. As the word "Presente" was repeated, we all felt the room fill as one by one our departed sisters and brothers filled the room and stood with us. We were welcoming the border crossers into our hearts, minds, doors, and spirits, and their spirits responded.

Notes

1. "How to Challenge U.S. Immigrant Detention and Deportation Policies," April 19, 2011, www.unitedmethodistwomen.org/act/alerts/item/index.cfm?id=508.
2. Children's Immigration Advocate, "100,000-plus Citizen Children Find Parents Deported," March 15th, 2011, http://childrenimmigrationadvocate. com/03/100000-plus-citizen-children-find-parents-deported.
3. Christine D. Pohl, *Making Room: Recovering Hospitality as a Christian Tradition* (Grand Rapids, MI: Wm. B. Eerdmans, 1999), 18–19.
4. John Wesley, "Sermon on the Mount," in *The Works of John Wesley, vol. 1: Sermons 1:1–33*, ed. Albert Outler (Nashville: Abingdon, 1984), 545–546.
5. Pohl, *Making Room*, 31.
6. John Calvin, *Commentary on the Prophet Isaiah*, vol. 1 (Grand Rapids: Wm. B. Eerdmans, 1948), 484.
7. Martin Luther King Jr., "Address to First Mass Meeting Montgomery Improvement Associationat Holt Street Baptist Church," December 5, 1955, http:// mlk-kpp01.stanford.edu/index.php/encyclopedia/documentsentry/the_addres_ to_the_first_montgomery_improvement_association_mia_mass_meeting.
8. Martin Luther King Jr., *Why We Can't Wait* (New York: Harper & Row, 1963), 67.
9. Dietrich Bonhoffer, *The Cost of Discipleship* (New York: Collier Books, 1937), 96.
10. Daniel L. Migliore, *Faith Seeking Understanding: An Introduction to Christian Theology* (Grand Rapids, MI: Wm.B. Eerdmans, 1991), 224–225.
11. Ibid., 225–226.
12. Daniel Homan and Lonni Collins Pratt, *Radical Hospitality: Benedict's Way of Love* (Brewster, MA: Paraclete Press, 2002), 73.
13. Pohl, *Making Room*, 12–13.
14. Homan and Pratt, *Radical Hospitality*, 224.
15. David Kirk, "Hospitality: Essence of Eastern Christian Lifestyle," *Diakonia* 16, no. 2 (1981): 112.

Chapter 8
History, Legislation, and Advocacy

Let love be genuine; hate what is evil, hold fast
to what is good; love one another with mutual
affection, outdo one another in showing honor. Do not
lag in zeal, be ardent in spirit, serve the Lord. Rejoice
in hope, be patient in suffering, persevere in prayer.
Contribute to the need of
the saints; extend hospitality to strangers.

—Romans 12:9–13

C urrent U.S. immigration history began in the sixteenth century with the arrival of the first explorers to North America. The Native Americans, who welcomed the newcomers, were decimated through violence and disease. Interestingly, the first settlers in what is now the United States were Spanish, so the Spanish speaking tradition can be traced to the first half of the sixteenth century. At that same time, European development began with the English.

In a 1992 article, Stephen Budansky projects what an "immigration interview report 28 DEC 1620" would have looked like. The article describes the hypothetical rejection of a boatload of "Gentlemen" from Holland. They would have been sent back because they were "not political refugees, but rather, economic refugees, merely out to better their lives."[1] However, they were not turned away, and

European settlements continued with no immigration laws for the next two hundred plus years.

Some settlers came to freely practice their religion. Many came to escape oppressive governments. In 1775 a successful Revolutionary War formed an independent nation. Early immigration looked much like the immigrant smuggling trade of today. Many people came as indentured workers and had to work for as long as five years to pay for their passage. In 1776, one-third of arriving immigrants were indentured workers.[2]

The eighteenth century found the Quakers and the Germans settling in to Pennsylvania, New Jersey, and Delaware. At that time, the Scotch-Irish settled in Western Pennsylvania and what would later become Kentucky and Tennessee. In addition, at least fifty thousand European convicts came to these shores to begin a new life. From these groups, the founders of this country rose to the surface.

It is important to note that although the founders almost universally believed in a divine creator, they worked very hard to ensure that there would be a definite division between church and state. The majority of them were Deists[3] who believed that God created the universe but does not remain involved in it. The United States, contrary to popular thought, was not developed to be a Christian nation. The government was to be separate from the church. People were to be free to worship as they chose. At the end of the eighteenth century only about 10 percent of the population attended church regularly.[4]

This division of church and state was necessary to ensure equality. However, there were some flaws in their thinking. Although the Declaration of Independence states, "We hold these truths to be self-evident, that all men are created equal," the words were not applicable to all residents of the land. They did not apply to Native Americans; African Americans were considered only three-fifths of a human being; and women were considered to be the property of their husbands. The struggle to obtain equality for all residents of the country continues to this day.

Immigration Law Time Line

The U.S. Constitution took effect in 1789. Since that time, immigration legislation has helped to define this nation. A timeline follows[5]:

- 1790—The Naturalization Act of 1790 permitted citizenship for "free white persons" living here for at least five years. (Until 1952, most nonwhite persons could not be naturalized.)
- 1798—The Naturalization Act of 1798 permitted the deportation of foreigners deemed dangerous and increased residency requirement to fourteen years. (It was revised in 1802, and the residency requirement decreased to five years.)
- 1848—The Treaty of Guadalupe Hidalgo ended the Mexican–American War. Eighty thousand Mexicans living in Texas, California, and the Southwest became citizens.
- 1875—the first exclusionary act barred convicts, prostitutes, and "coolies" (Chinese contract laborers). The Immigration Act of 1882 expanded the list to include paupers and "mental defectives."
- 1882—The Chinese Exclusion Act was the first immigration law. It kept Chinese laborers out of the country for ten years and extended the color line.
- 1882—The Immigration Act of 1882 levied a tax of fifty cents on all immigrants.
- 1885—The Alien Contract Labor Law prohibited bringing foreigners in under contract for labor. Exceptions were domestic workers and skilled workers to establish a new trade or industry.

- 1891—Congress extended immigration ineligibility to persons suffering from a loathsome or a dangerous contagious disease, persons convicted of a misdemeanor of moral turpitude, and polygamists.
- 1891—Office of Immigration was created as part of the U.S. Treasury. It was later moved to the U.S. Justice Department as the Immigration and Naturalization Service (INS). In 2003, it was moved to the Department of Homeland Security, which is divided into U.S. Citizenship and Immigration Services (CIS), U.S. Customs and Border Protection (CBP), and U.S. Immigration and Customs Enforcement (ICE).
- 1892—The Geary Act extended the Chinese Exclusion Act for ten more years and required Chinese residents to carry permits at all times.
- 1892—Ellis Island opened after the federal government took over the responsibility of controlling immigration. Immigrants made up 15 percent of the nation.
- 1901—The Anarchist Exclusion Act prohibited the entry of persons judged to be political extremists or anarchists. (President McKinley had been assassinated by a Polish anarchist on September 14, 1901.)
- 1902—Chinese Exclusion Act renewed with no ending date.
- 1906—The Naturalization Act of 1906 created standardized naturalization requirements including some knowledge of English.
- 1907—The Expatriation Act revoked the citizenship of an American woman who married a foreign national.
- 1907—A "gentleman's agreement" between the United States and Japan curtailed Japanese immigration to the United States and increased taxes on new immigrants.

- 1917—The Immigration Act of 1917 created an "Asiatic Barred Zone" that restricted immigration from Asia.
- 1917—The Jones-Shaffroth Act granted citizenship to Puerto Ricans.
- 1922—The Cable Act repealed part of the Expatriation Act. However, an American woman who married an Asian man still lost her citizenship.
- 1924—The Oriental Exclusion Act prohibited most Asian immigration, including that of foreign-born wives and children of U.S. citizens.
- 1940—Congress allowed all women to repatriate who had lost citizenship by marriage between 1907 and 1922.
- 1929—National Origins Act set a ceiling of 150,000 immigrants, with 70 percent from northern and western Europe and the other 30 percent from the Western Hemisphere.
- 1942—The Bracero Program was initiated based on the need for agricultural workers. The program lasted until 1965 and provided temporary employment for close to 4.5 million Mexicans.
- 1943—Chinese Exclusion Act repealed.
- 1948—Displaced Persons Act permitted 400,000 persons displaced by World War II to enter the country provided they passed a security check, had employment and housing, and did not threaten U.S. citizens' jobs and homes.
- 1952—McCarran-Walter Act consolidated earlier immigration laws and removed race as a reason for exclusion. It also added political ideology to the admission criterion. Persons who were communists or former Nazis could be excluded.
- 1965—The Immigration Act was amended. It established a ceiling of 170,000 immigrants from the Eastern Hemisphere and 120,000 from the Western Hemisphere and abolished quotas based on nationality.

- 1978—Worldwide immigration ceiling of 290,000 replaced separate hemisphere ceilings.
- 1980—Refugee Act developed a separate immigration classification based on refugee definition. The president was given the authority to set an annual ceiling on refugees and the power to admit any group of refugees in case of emergency.
- 1986—Immigration Reform and Control Act raised the annual immigration ceiling to 540,000. Amnesty was given to undocumented aliens who could prove they had been in the United States continually since January 1, 1982. Stiff sanctions were put in place for hiring undocumented workers. (The government rarely enforced these stiff sanctions, which resulted in companies being free to hire and recruit undocumented workers. Had the law been followed the United States would not have had more than ten million undocumented immigrants at the beginning of the twenty-first century.)
- 1990—Immigration Act of 1990 raised the immigration ceiling for two years and then dropped it to 675,000 per year. It granted ten thousand permanent visas per year to immigrants who would invest $1 million in business in urban areas or $500,000 in rural areas and create at least ten jobs.
- 1996—Illegal Immigration Reform and Immigrant Responsibility Act established measures to control U.S. borders, protect legal workers through worksite enforcement, and remove criminal and other deportable aliens. There were no penalties for companies that hired undocumented workers. It also expanded the definition of aggravated felon, reformed exclusion and deportation procedures, streamlined the expedited removal process to speed deportation and exclusion, and expanded immigration detention.

- 2001—USA PATRIOT Act (Uniting and Strengthening America by Providing Appropriate Tools Required to Intercept and Obstruct Terrorism Act of 2001) gave the Executive Branch sweeping new powers. The act permits noncitizens to be jailed solely on suspicion and to deny readmission to the United States for engaging in antigovernment speech. Noncitizen suspects can be detained in six-month increments indefinitely without judicial review.
- 2003—The 1990 International Convention on the Protection of the Rights of All Migrant Workers and Members of Their Families entered into force. Its primary objective is to protect migrant workers and their families.
- 2003—The Immigration Act of 1990 was changed and transferred the authority to designate, extend, or terminate Temporary Protected Status (TPS) from the Attorney General to the Secretary of Homeland Security.
- 2005—The REAL ID Act, which used the driver's license as a national identity card and greatly decreased the possibilities of gaining asylum in the United States, passed for implementation in May 2011.
- 2010 Arizona S.B. 1070 made it a crime not to carry proof of legal residency. This encouraged racial profiling, harassment, and discrimination against Latinos. This state law was challenged as unconstitutional and also became the basis for copycat legislation in other states, including Alabama in 2011.

Immigration Reform

In 2011, humane immigration reform that will seriously alter the treatment of the immigrants in this land is needed that will provide a path to legalization, protect families, protect the rights of all workers, reform inhumane detention and deportation processes, and make the visa system more efficient. Two other key bills have been active for many years. They are the Ag Jobs Bill and the DREAM Act.

The Agricultural Job Opportunities, Benefits and Security Act of 2009 (Ag Jobs) would create an earned adjustment program enabling several hundred thousand H-2A guest workers and undocumented farmworkers to obtain temporary immigration status with the possibility of becoming permanent residents of the United States. In 2011 it was introduced into Congress, and on June 22 as part of Senate bill 1258 Comprehensive Immigration Reform Act of 2011.

The Development, Relief, and Education for Alien Minors (DREAM) Act is bipartisan legislation that would permit high school graduates who were brought to the United States as children and have lived here for at least five years to apply for temporary legal status. If approved, these students would be able to make their status permanent by attending college or serving in the military for at least two years. It would also eliminate a federal provision that discourages states from providing in-state tuition to immigrant students. United Methodist Women supports the passage of the DREAM act. For more information, visit www.unitedmethodistwomen.org/act/immigration.

Secure Communities is an administratively created deportation program that relies on federal, state, and local law enforcement agencies to identify and remove serious criminal offenders. It was piloted in 2008 and has been used since 2009. It has not been congressionally mandated. The program has created a great deal of controversy as it is seen to be used as a general deportation tool by many states and localities. Many U.S. citizen children have seen parents with no criminal records deported, and it has had a detrimental effect on immigrants, residents, and law enforcement agencies. Humane immigration reform is vital to the political, social, and economic health of the United States. The Population Bureau "Immigration Update 2010" indicated that with a total U.S. population of 310 million in 2010, 40 million persons (or 13 percent) were foreign born. According to the Migration Policy Institute, in 2007, the top seven countries represented were Mexico, the Philippines, India, China, El Salvador, Vietnam, and Korea. In that year, there were 1 million Koreans, who made up 2.7 percent of all immigrants and accounted for 2 percent of all undocumented immigrants in the United States.[6]

The Department of Homeland Security estimates that there were 10.5 million undocumented immigrants in 2011. This includes foreign students, diplomats, and temporary workers. Some estimates claim that about one million return home each year. The largest percentage of undocumented immigrants come from Central America; however, others come from Asia, Africa, Europe, and the Caribbean. In addition, although they are often thought to be persons who have crossed the border between the United States and Mexico, more than 40 percent of the undocumented immigrants arrived with visas permitting them to be in the United States for a specific reason (travel, work, or study being the most common).[7] When those visas expired, they simply remained in the country. However, undocumented persons of European, Canadian, or Australian descent rarely have their immigration status questioned. Skin color, unfortunately, is often the driving factor in questioning someone's immigration status.

The xenophobia surrounding immigrants in this country has resulted in the detention of immigrants being the fastest growing and most lucrative prison industry in the United States. This along with the intricate and constantly changing immigration laws and regulations has resulted in a great need for legal assistance for all immigrants.

Justice for Our Neighbors

Care for the plight of immigrants and their many legal concerns was the impetus for the development of Justice for Our Neighbors (JFON), which holds monthly clinics in twelve states providing free professional legal services to immigrants. The program connects church-based, volunteer immigration clinics to immigrants and asylum seekers who need help in navigating the complex immigration laws of the land. JFON was developed by the United Methodist Committee on Relief (UMCOR) and offers radical, inclusive hospitality to immigrants and their families. Local volunteers welcome the immigrants to the monthly clinics and respond to the legal needs of immigrants seeking to reunify their families, secure immigration status, and enjoy the right to work.

The radical, inclusive hospitality offered by JFON affects not only immigrants but also the volunteers and people who learn about it. Nori, a JFON volunteer, wrote, "I just wanted to let you know what an impact JFON—even my minimal involvement (i.e., merely being on the e-mail distribution list) has been on my life . . . this is the first time ever that I have thought about coming back to the church and I am also encouraged there are people in the Methodist church that care about immigrants. I mean WOW!"

United Methodist Women Work for Immigrant Rights

Migrant and Civil Rights in the United States as well as global migration are focus areas for social action by United Methodist Women, with a particular concern for migrant women, youth and children. The initiative understands immigration as a racial justice issue that gives continuity to the civil rights movement and claims for indigenous rights in the ongoing national debate about which communities are included as part of our national fabric. In the United States, United Methodist Women members advocate for immigrant rights by supporting accompanying immigrants in their communities, legislative reform, speaking out against unfair laws and policies, visiting detention centers, participating in the DREAM fast to support passage of the DREAM Act, organizing public witnesses, educating themselves on global migration, and educating others on immigrant and civil rights. Globally, United Methodist Women has participated in United Nations meetings, in the intergovernmental Global Forum on Migration and Development, and in the People's Global Action on Migration, Development, and Human Rights, a migrant-led global forum. United Methodist Women provides various practical resources for members and partners. Join this work that welcomes the stranger and treats all as neighbors at www.united-methodistwomen.org/act/immigration, immigration.umwonline.net, and facebook.com/groups/umwimmigration.

The Women's Division of the General Board of Global Ministries of The United Methodist Church wrote and adopted A Charter for Racial Justice in 1978, which in 1980 was adopted by the entire denomination, strengthening the mandate to work for racial justice within jurisdiction, conference, district and local structures. This charter, which can be found at www.unitedmethodistwomen.org/resources/racialjustice/charter, serves as the basis for United Methodist Women racial justice work. United Methodist Women has worked with the United Methodist Task Force on Immigration and other United Methodist agencies to draft and introduce other migrant rights' legislation adopted by The United Methodist Church, such as "Global Migration and the Quest for Justice" and "Welcoming the Migrant to the United States," both found in *The Book of Resolutions of The United Methodist Church*, 2008. At the 2012 General Conference of The United Methodist Church, the policymaking body of the denomination, United Methodist Women will be introducing legislation calling for the end to racial profiling and anti-immigrant laws. The resolution, titled "The Criminalization of Communities of Color in the United States," states, "The United Methodist Church needs to actively work to dismantle current policies that depict whole groups of people as criminals and that respond with profiling and mass incarceration."

God's Law or Human's Law?

Immigrants are now and have always been an integral part of the United States, whose identity is wrapped up in the colorful combination of cultures from around the world. It is the diversity of this country that has made it a world leader. It is crucial that diversity continue to be embraced and that doors remain open for orderly immigration to the United States. It is necessary for everyone to actively participate in the development of immigration reform for the country to maintain its identity, to continue to embrace its traditional values of welcoming the stranger, and to maintain its place as a leader of the free world. As the immigration reform debate continues, immigrants are increasingly blamed for the woes of this country. As anti-immigrant legislation and regulations are formulated, Romans 13:1–7 and how it is understood takes on great importance. It is often used as the main biblical text to support deporting all undocumented persons in the United States. On the surface, it seems to say that God has put our governing authorities in power, and we are to be "law abiding citizens" doing whatever they tell us. As concerned citizens and Christians we ask, do we follow God's law or human's law? Read Romans 13:1–7:

> Let every person be subject to the governing authorities; for there is no authority except from God, and those authorities that exist have been instituted by God. Therefore whoever resists authority resists what God has ap-

pointed, and those who resist will incur judgment. For rulers are not a terror to good conduct, but to bad. Do you wish to have no fear of the authority? Then do what is good, and you will receive its approval; for it is God's servant for your good. But if you do what is wrong, you should be afraid, for the authority does not bear the sword in vain! It is the servant of God to execute wrath on the wrongdoer. Therefore one must be subject, not only because of wrath but also because of conscience. For the same reason you also pay taxes, for the authorities are God's servants, busy with this very thing. Pay to all what is due them—taxes to whom taxes are due, revenue to whom revenue is due, respect to whom respect is due, honor to whom honor is due.

This passage can be troubling for Christians who understand inclusive hospitality to strangers as one of the key biblical mandates. Therefore, it is important to look at this and all scripture through a variety of lenses, as the first response to a text may only scratch the surface of the text.

A literal interpretation of Romans 13:1 calls for citizens to let the government have its way on immigration issues because scripture tells us God has put the governing authorities in power; therefore, the law of the land takes precedence. A more thorough study of the scriptures will show a very different viewpoint. Many Christians believe that often God's law of love takes precedence over the law of the land. Hopefully, a thorough and prayerful study of this scripture will result in an understanding that can be embraced by followers of Christ on all sides of the issue.

The passage "for there is no authority except from God, and those authorities that exist have been instituted by God" literally means that every "authority" since the beginning of time (good or bad, honest or corrupt) has been put in power by God. This is a challenge, as the text advises us not to resist authority and states that those who resist authority will incur judgment because rulers are not a terror to good conduct but to bad conduct. It is very troubling to be told that God has put authorities in power who persecute or exclude large groups from being accepted and integrated into a society.

Groups in power can use this passage to affirm their position, and the marginalized can see it as a way for persons in authority to further their disenfranchisement. It is also dangerous to advocates for justice, as it can be an excuse for inaction. Simply stated, it can be interpreted: God puts people in power. We must accept both God's decisions and their actions. Verse 4 reads, "It [the government] is God's servant for your good." This permits the recipients of good to thank God and ignore the rest of the world, feeling that because of their exclusive relationship with God, they are being blessed.

This is perhaps the most dangerous aspect of Christianity, the viewpoint that Christians are superior to others and chosen by God because their belief is right and the rest of the world is wrong. (Unfortunately, it is also not uncommon for branches of Christianity to believe only their form of Christianity is acceptable to God.)

By looking closely at the words and actions of Jesus, we see that he was an activist seeking justice for the "other": the marginalized, the foreigners, the gentiles, the children, the migrant workers, and the oppressed of his day. Rather than following authority, Jesus often challenged authority. In fact, his crucifixion was a result of his demanding justice and fairness for the marginalized people who flocked to him. One might say that his actions were in direct opposition to many of the words of this passage. He did not see himself as a "subject" of the governing or to the religious authorities. He repeatedly spoke out against both groups and was feared for his outspokenness and actions.

If we accept, "Therefore whoever resists authority resists what God has appointed, and those who resist will incur judgment. For rulers are not a terror to good conduct, but to bad," we can easily take the next step and say Jesus got what he asked for. He resisted authority, he incurred judgment, and he was punished. In fact the passage goes on to say, "If you do what is wrong, you should be afraid, for the authority does not bear the sword in vain! It is the servant of God to execute wrath on the wrongdoer."

The authorities did just that. They crucified Jesus. If he was crucified because he resisted the authority of the governing authorities and they are "a terror not to good conduct but to bad," it would follow that the crucifixion of Jesus was a deserved punishment for his bad conduct. He was the wrongdoer! (The Roman and Jewish authorities would argue this was the reason for his crucifixion.) However, we know that Jesus' death was for the redemption of the world and because his preferential option for the poor was a threat to those in power.

One might argue that according to this passage God gave those in power the authority to crucify Jesus to carry out God's plan to use his son for the redemption of the world. However, that argument breaks down at the level of their being in power because they are given authority by God to execute justice on the wrongdoer. If Jesus did no wrong (a universally accepted Christian teaching) then the call to blindly accept all rulers as having authority from God disintegrates. If they were in fact acting as instruments of God, we should then give those who crucified Jesus the highest respect and thanks. They, along with Jesus, should be seen as instruments of salvation. But to do this requires our also seeing Jesus as the wrongdoer in the scenario. Hence the difficulty encountered in blindly following the laws of the land. They must always be viewed in context and in comparison and contrast to the laws of God.

The importance of following the laws of the land is held in high esteem in many churches. In fact, national flags can be found in the front of many churches attesting to the blurring of the lines between church and state. Although this is a far cry from separation of church and state, it reaffirms the belief that a good Christian is a good citizen, and God has blessed the citizens of this country for their special connection with God. Therefore, the Christians of the United States are to be an exclusive community rather than an inclusive community. They are to follow the instructions of the leaders and see to it that we remain a "Christian" nation and that only "approved" outsiders can enter our gates. This viewpoint makes it difficult for many Christians to see any other interpretation of scriptures and makes advocacy for immigrants very, very difficult.

The United States is considered by many to be a "Christian" nation. The fact that the founding fathers were for the most part Deists seems to have been expunged from the religious history books, as has the practice of separating church and state, unless it suits our particular agendas. In addition, the government continues to exclude more and more people. This causes a conflict in Romans 13, which makes some scholars wonder whether or not verses 1 to 7 were a later addition to the original scripture.

Romans 12 gives instruction on proper conduct and living lives of love, stating in verses 11–13, "Do not lag in zeal, be ardent in spirit, serve the Lord. Rejoice in hope, be patient in suffering, persevere in prayer. Contribute to the needs of the saints; extend hospitality to strangers." It ends with verse 21, "Do not be overcome by evil, but overcome evil with good."

Romans 13 begins with the admonition to be subject to governing authorities, a diversion from the previous thought. However, if one skips to verses 8 through 10, they read, "Owe no one anything, except to love one another, for the one who loves another has fulfilled the law. The commandments . . . are summed up in this word,

'Love your neighbor as yourself.' Love does no wrong to a neighbor; therefore, love is the fulfilling of the law."

It seems that the scriptural passages preceding Romans 13:1–7 and those following it are in contradiction to that particular passage and in fact advocate a response that will very often be in conflict with the governing authorities laws, actions, and regulations. Therefore, it is most important that the question always be asked, "Is the action of the government in keeping with or in opposition to God's law of love?"

This is crucial in the treatment of refugees, asylum seekers, immigrants, and migrants. Scriptures make it quite clear that foreigners are our neighbors, and hospitality to strangers is a recurrent theme throughout the Bible. However, instead of caring for them, we are closing borders to them, imprisoning them, shooting them at our southern border, forcing them into the desert where many die, sending them back, and using them as indentured servants and slaves. So we read the passage closely to seek clues for understanding it in the twenty-first century.

The passage differs slightly in terminology in a variety of translations, which are basically in agreement. Two use the term *soul* and the other two use *person* or *persons*. Eugene Peterson's *The Message* uses the term *citizen* and adds a qualifying statement, "All governments are under God. Insofar as there is peace and order. It's God's order." This makes it much more palatable for persons who are concerned when the governing authorities seem to be acting against the very core of God's message, as they did with the crucifixion of Christ.

This core message, which is so often overlooked, is found in Romans 13:8–10:

> Owe no one anything, except to love one another; for the
> one who loves another has fulfilled the law. The com-

mandments "You shall not commit adultery; You shall not murder; You shall not steal; You shall not covet"; and any other commandment, are summed up in this word, "Love your neighbor as yourself." Love does no wrong to a neighbor; therefore, love is the fulfilling of the law.

The two passages—one right after the other—are so very conflicting when we see rampant mistreatment of disenfranchised persons in our society and the blatant ignoring of verses 8 through 10 by both the citizens and the government. This demonstrates that there is a tendency to selectively embrace scripture. This passage has to be taken in context with the previous passage that is the key to exactly how and when we should follow the authorities.

The New Oxford Annotated Bible says that Romans, an instrument of moral instruction and exhortation, is "a sustained appeal for holy living, directed to Gentile Christians, tempted to look down on their beleaguered Jewish neighbors, within the Christian congregations and without. The apostle's call to realize in common life the justice of God which the Christian congregation celebrates is the letter's enduring legacy."[8]

The Book of Romans was written about CE 57 during a period of relative political stability. It was after the Jews, who had been expelled from the capital, returned. This may have caused tensions between the Gentile and Jewish Christians, as the Gentile Christian house churches had become predominant. The writer wanted to prevent any civic disturbances in Rome that might make the Jewish population vulnerable. Therefore the admonition to be subject to governing authorities seems somewhat in contrast to Paul's overriding belief in a universal accountability to God. However, this passage seems to be strategically located between two passages that temper what he writes and seems to be in agreement with the translation, mentioned earlier, found in *The Message*: "Be a good citizen. All governments are under God insofar as there is peace and order. It's God's order. So live responsibly as a citizen." Note the qualification in this translation, "Insofar as there is peace and order. It's God's order." This idea of God's order frames the difficult passage of Romans 13:1–7.

Greg Herrick quotes James Kallas, writing in an article "Romans xiii. 1–7: An Interpolation," in which he claims that Roman 13:1–7 is a later insertion into the text. He says this because he feels that it is well known that the ending of the epistle has been altered and this is the only place where Paul comments on Christian relationships to civil authorities. He also states that the passage is isolated, having no real connection to what comes before and after it. In addition, he states that it "contradicts basic Pauline ideas and basic Pauline forms of expression."[9]

However, a very similar train of thought is seen in 1 Peter 2:13–17:

> For the Lord's sake accept the authority of every human institution, whether of the emperor as supreme, or of governors, as sent by him to punish those who do wrong and to praise those who do right. For it is God's will that by doing right you should silence the ignorance of the foolish. As servants of God, live as free people, yet do not use your freedom as a pretext for evil. Honor everyone. Love the family of believers. Fear God. Honor the Emperor.

Both this passage and the passage in Romans argue that Christians are to recognize world leaders and governmental authorities. It can also be argued we are to do so only if recognizing and responding to them does not negate a Christian's first allegiance to God and the command to Love. John Wesley supported this thought when he stated that "the powers that be are appointed by God—It might be rendered, are subordinate to, or, orderly disposed under, God;

implying, that they are God's deputies or vice-regents and consequently, their authority being, in effect, his, demands our conscientious obedience."[10]

In analyzing this thought it becomes obvious that once the "powers that be" stray from acting according to God's teachings, it is most important for Christians to take the stand that Peter takes in Acts 5:29, when he states, "We must obey God rather than any human authority."

This is the central issue of the passage, the central issue for the Roman community, and the central issue for Christian followers of Christ in the twenty-first century. God-given authority is meant to be used by the authorities in power to carry out the will of God. At the time this was written, the community was functioning with the ancient scriptures and felt that the state had to function within its God-given ordering or it would be judged by God. So just as the placement of the text would have caused first century Christians to pause and ponder just how much submission to authorities was required, it should also cause us to pause and ponder just how much submission to authorities is required.

As we look at the world locally, regionally, nationally, and internationally, we see many Christians in the United States becoming known for their acts of hatred and exclusivity as they embrace the laws and regulations of the present governing authorities and encourage this country to close its borders and selectively exclude many of the least the last and the lost of the world. It is crucially important to educate and advocate for the marginalized in our society. It is also important to counteract the media messages that present Christianity with a face of hate by showing the face of love, which in reality is the face of God, Christ, the Holy Spirit and the great majority of Christians.

It becomes ever more important to look at scriptures contextually and refuse to accept interpretations that, on the surface, seem so obvious when taken out of context as this passage does. We must do all we can to reclaim a church where the words and teachings of the nonviolent, all-inclusive, welcoming Christ are the driving force of its existence.

In 2005, John Dear, a Jesuit priest, wrote an article titled "Pharisee Nation." In it he states,

> We have become a culture of Pharisees. Instead of practicing an authentic spirituality of compassion, nonviolence, love and peace, we as a collective people have become self-righteous, arrogant, powerful, murderous hypocrites who dominate and kill others in the name of God. . . . This spirituality of empire insists that violence saves us, might makes right, war is justified, bombing raids are blessed, nuclear weapons offer the only true security from terrorism, and the good news is not love for our enemies, but the elimination of them. . . . Our Pharisee rulers would have us believe that our wars and our weapons are holy and blessed by God.[11]

Passages like this cause us to ask: Are we putting our faith in power structures or are we putting our faith in God and seeking to spread Christ's gospel of peace? As advocates for immigrants and refugees, and peace, it is imperative to live fully as disciples of Christ and both embrace and work to help others to embrace the nonviolent Jesus of the gospels. His all-inclusive love was the hallmark of ancient Christianity, which lived out his teachings and welcomed the strangers.

By 2011, the Interfaith Immigration Coalition, www.interfaith immigration.org, made up of hundreds of faith-based groups, including Christians, Jews, Muslims, Buddhists, Baha'is, Hindus, Sikhs, and others, have, in addition to continuing to seek just, fair immigration reform, come together to define their beliefs and call for action. They state,

> We call for immigration reform because each day in our congregations, service programs, health-care facilities, and schools we witness the human consequences of a broken and outdated system. We see the exploitation of undocumented workers and the plight of separated families, as well as the escalation of community fear due to indiscriminate raids and local police acting as federal immigration agents. Humane immigration reform would help put an end to this suffering, which offends the dignity of all human beings. The Hebrew Bible states: "The strangers who sojourn with you shall be to you as the natives among you, and you shall love them as yourself; for you were strangers in the land of Egypt" (Leviticus 19:33–34). In the New Testament, Jesus says "what you do to the least of my brethren, you do unto me" (Matthew 25:40). The Qur'an tells us that we should "do good to . . . those in need, neighbors who are near, neighbors who are strangers, the companion by your side, the wayfarer that you meet" (4:36). The Hindu Taitiriya Upanishad tells us: "The guest is a representative of God" (1.11.2).[12]

Concern about immigration is a universal faith-based concern, and people of all faiths make up the United States. As the face of the nation continues to change, and it will in spite of massive efforts to stop it from happening, it becomes ever more important for the church to remember that Jesus said he came to serve not to be served. Most important, we must look to Jesus, who taught us that those who will inherit the kingdom will be those who cared for the hungry, the thirsty, the stranger, the naked, the sick, and the prisoner and who discovered that the person they were really caring for was none other than Jesus the Christ—the stranger in our midst.

United Methodist Stance on Immigration

Jesus was willing to stand up to the powers that be and seek justice for the marginalized and oppressed. We are called to do the same. For this reason the United Methodist Church has taken a stance on immigration reform. Part of United Methodist Resolution 3281, "Welcoming the Migrant to the United States," found in the 2008 *Book of Resolutions of The United Methodist Church*, is included here because of its importance in helping guide and direct our missions and ministries.

> A Call to Action
>
> The United Methodist Church affirms the worth, dignity, and inherent value and rights of all persons regardless of their nationality or legal status. United Methodist churches throughout the United States are urged to build bridges with migrants in their local communities, to learn from them, celebrate their presence in the United States and recognize and appreciate the contributions in all areas of life that migrants bring. We call upon all United Methodist churches to engage in the following:
>
> - Advocate for legislation that will uphold the civil and human rights of all migrants.
> - Begin English as a second language classes as part of a ministry to migrant communities.
> - Denounce and oppose the rise of xenophobic, racist, violent reactions against migrants.

- Oppose the building of a wall between the United States and Mexico.
- Call the U.S. government to immediately cease all arrests, detainment, and deportations of undocumented immigrants, including children, solely based upon their immigration status.
- Provide wherever possible pastoral care and crisis intervention to refugees and newly arrived migrants.
- Work with civic and legal organizations to support migrant communities affected by harsh immigration laws and overreaching national security measures.
- Support churches that prayerfully choose to offer sanctuary to undocumented migrants.
- Continue the work of the Immigration Task Force.[13]

In addition, The United Methodist Church is urged to advocate for just, fair reform of the U.S. immigration system. Any legislation to reform to the U.S. immigration system must affirm the worth, dignity, and inherent value and rights of migrants and must also include an opportunity for legal status for all undocumented migrants; a clearing of the backlogs and reunifying families separated by migration or detainment; an increase in the number of visas for short-term workers to come into the United States; the protections of all workers who come to stay for a certain period of time as well as for those who stay permanently; elimination of privately operated detention centers, which are not regulated by the federal or state governments[*]; elimination of indefinite detention, incarceration of

---

[*] In the 2004 *Book of Resolutions of The United Methodist Church*, Resolution 257, "Prison Industrial Complex," states that "many states where private prisons are now operating have no laws regulating their operations (including health, safety, security, legal access for prisoners, and disciplinary policies). Many private prisons are under no obligation to ensure access to information about prisoners held in them or how they are classified, and often regard this as proprietary information."

children, and the expanding prison population, which also benefits privately owned detention centers and prisons; and preservation of due process and access to courts and to adequate legal representation for all migrants regardless of legal status.

United Methodist Women embrace the *Book of Resolution* statement and have an immigration initiative as part of its ongoing commitment to racial justice and civil and human rights. The biblical mandate to "welcome the stranger" has long been the foundation of The United Methodist Church's policy statements and outreach to immigrant communities in the United States. Likewise, United Methodist Women seeks to welcome immigrants and advocate for just immigration policies. As mentioned, this initiative is another effort to fulfill A Charter for Racial Justice, declare racism a sin, and dismantle institutional racism. United Methodist Women extends a welcoming hand to immigrant communities and call on all churches and communities to develop a radical, inclusive hospitality that embraces all people without regard to immigration status. Help is needed to make this a reality. Will we, working together, build radical, inclusive, hospitable communities and hold out the healing hands of Christ to our world? Let us ask our God to change us. Change us that God's will may be done on earth as it is in heaven.

Notes

1. Stephen Budansky, "1620 to 1992: Long Ago but Not So Far Away (Imaginary Reaction of Boat People in 1620)," *U.S. News and World Report* 112, no. 22 (1992): 22.

2. Deanna Barker, "Indentured Servitude in Colonial America," Mert Sahingolu, http://mertsahinoglu.com/research/indentured-servitude-colonial-america.

3. Jim Peterson, "The Revolution of Belief," 2007, www.earlyamericanhistory.net/founding_fathers.htm.

4. Gordon S. Wood, *The Radicalism of the American Revolution* (New York: Vintage Books, 1993).

5. Compiled from various sources, including PBS, "For Educators: Immigration Policy: Past and Present, www.pbs.org/independentlens/newamericans/for

educators_lesson_plan_03.html; Digital History, "Landmarks in Immigration History," www.digitalhistory.uh.edu/historyonline/immigration_chron.cfm; "History of Immigration to the United States," *Wikipedia*, http://en.wikipedia.org/wiki/Immigration_History_to_United_States; "Cable Act," *Wikipedia*, http://en.wikipedia.org/wiki/Cable_Act.

6. Aaron Terrazas and Cristina Batag, "Korean Immigrants in the United States," Migration Policy Institute, January 2009, www.migrationinformation.org/USfocus/display.cfm?ID=793.

7. Ted Robbins, "Nearly Half of Illegal Immigrants Overstay Visas," *All Things Considered*, June 14, 2006, www.npr.org/templates/story/story.php?storyId=5485917.

8. Michael D. Coogan, ed., "The Letter of Paul to the ROMANS," in *The New Oxford Annotated Bible*, 3rd edition, NRSV (New York: Oxford University Press, 2001).

9. Greg Herrick, "Paul and Civil Disobedience in Romans 13:1–7," in *The Net Bible* (Richardson, TX: Biblical Studies Press, 1997), http://bible.org/article/paul-and-civil-obedience-romans-131-7.

10. John Wesley, "Explanatory Notes on the Whole Bible," www.biblestudytools.com/commentaries/wesleys-explanatory-notes.

11. John Dear, "Pharisee Nation," CommonDreams.org, February 15, 2005, www.commondreams.org/views05/0215-21.htm.

12. "Interfaith Statement in Support of Immigration Reform," October 24, 2008, www.interfaithimmigration.org/wp-content/uploads/2008/10/interfaith-cir-statement-final2.pdf.

13. "Welcoming the Migrant to the US," Resolution 3281, *The Book of Resolutions of The United Methodist Church*, 2008, 418–419.

EPILOGUE

The royal Roman court rang with laughter. Mary Magdelene was terrified; she had spoken the truth. She had not expected this response. The Emperor Tiberius chortled, jumped from his throne, and rushed down the steps. He pushed Mary to the floor, shouting, "That's preposterous! Jesus could no more rise from the dead than—" Stopping, he looked around. All eyes were on him. Mary was huddled on the floor, afraid to look up. He whirled toward the table, grabbed a hardboiled egg, and exclaimed, "Jesus could no more rise from the dead than . . . this egg turn red!"

With that, he raised his arm. His huge hand obscured the white egg. Tiberius smiled, turned around to make sure all eyes were on him, and slowly opened his hand. Everyone gasped and backed away! Mary felt a chill. Without looking, she knew what had happened. The egg had turned red at his words of doubt—as red as the blood of Jesus. The emperor was frozen in fear, his hand still extended. His expression was that of terror. He was unsure of what to do, where to turn, or where to place the egg. So many thoughts raced through his mind. A still, small voice, one that he did not want to acknowledge, whispered, "She speaks the truth. I have risen from the dead." Confusion spread across his face. No one moved.

A still, small voice whispered to Mary, "They will know the truth that will set them free. You are the bearer of the truth. Rise slowly and reach for the egg. You will know what to do." With the grace of an angel, she stood and was eye level with the emperor. They were alone in the center of the room. Slowly she held out her hand.

Slowly he lowered his arm. For a split second she was terrified that he might throw or drop the egg, but he did neither. He stepped toward Mary and handed her the blood red egg. She accepted the egg with the palm of her right hand, looked into his eyes, covered his hand with her left hand, and said so only Tiberius could hear, "You will know the truth and the truth will set you free. This egg is your freedom. The messiah died willingly that you might live." Her gaze did not leave his; she knew that in his heart he knew the truth. His fingers grasped the egg. Softly she asked, "Will you accept Christ's freedom?" An indescribable sadness filled his eyes as he painfully looked away. Still holding the egg, he turned, placed it in the center of the table, said nothing, and returned to his throne.

Everyone in the court knew instinctively it was best to leave quickly and quietly. Mary Magdelene followed the silent crowd. Her head was spinning, her heart was pounding with joy, her mind was reeling, and she was humbled. She knew the truth would set the world free and marveled that she had been chosen to be the first to see the risen Lord and that she, a woman, was one of the leaders of the disciples who were to share the gospel throughout the world. So much had happened since the day Jesus had freed her of seven demons. So much had happened since she had joined his inner circle of disciples. Oh, so much had happened since his crucifixion and resurrection. And now—this!

Everyone in the room knew the truth of Christ's resurrection. How many would accept this truth and act on it? There was the question. She knew Jesus had whispered to everyone gathered. "I am the way the truth and the life. You will know the truth and the truth will set you free!" Mary knew he had also offered a radical inclusive invitation to each, calling quietly, "You . . . you . . . you, follow me." How many she wondered would accept that invitation? How many across history would accept that invitation she pondered. It was not for her to know.

She heard footsteps behind her and turned. No one was there, and then she knew. Christ was with her. An unseen hand grasped hers and she knew the meaning of the words "we are one in the spirit, we are one in the Lord." Mary knew that Christ would walk with her into eternity. Slowly she looked at her hands knowing that for every being she touched, her hands would be Christ's hand reaching out to the world. She was but one part of the newly born body of Christ. (*Author's version of an ancient Orthodox Christian narrative.*)

BIBLIOGRAPHY

Adeney, Miriam. "Colorful Initiatives: North American Diasporas in Mission." *Missiology: An International Review* XXXIX, no. 1 (January 2011).

Adherents.com. "Major Religions of the World Ranked by Number of Adherents." Modified August 9, 2007. www.adherents.com/Religions_By_Adherents.html.

Amnesty International USA. *United States of America: Lost in the Labyrinth: Detention of Asylum-Seekers.* New York: AIUSA, 1999.

Appleby, Jerry. *Missions Have Come Home to America.* Kansas City, MO: Nazarene, 1986.

Barker, Deanna. "Indentured Servitude in Colonial America." MertSahingolu. http://mertsahinoglu.com/research/indentured-servitude-colonial-america.

Barton, Carol. "Race and Migration: Ten Years after Durban." September 2011, www.unitedmethodistwomen.org/news/articles/item/index.cfm?id=663.

Berry, M. F., and J. W. Blassingame. *Long Memory: The Black Experience in America.* Sixth edition revised. New York: Oxford University Press, 1982.

Bloomberg, Michael R., Mayor, City of New York. Testimony before the Committee on the Judiciary. United States Senate. June 5, 2006.

Bninski, Carolyn. "Challenge Mantras for War." April 22, 2005. Rocky Mountain Peace and Justice Center. www.rmpjc.org.

Bondi, Roberta. *To Love As God Loves: Conversations with the Early Church*. Minneapolis: Fortress Press, 1991.

Bonhoeffer, Dietrich. *The Cost of Discipleship*. New York: Collier Books, 1937.

Bonhoeffer, Dietrich. *Life Together: A Discussion of Christian Fellowship*. New York: Harper & Row, 1954.

Border Working Group. *Stop Border Deaths Now!* Washington, DC: Border Working Group, 2005.

Bread for the World Institute. "Institute Notes: Unauthorized Immigration, Hunger, and Poverty." September 2010. www.bread.org/institute/research/fact-sheets/unauthorized-immigration_hunger-and-povety.pdf.

Brussat, Frederic, and Mary Ann Brussat. "Film Review: *Dirty Pretty Things*." www.spiritualityandpractice.com/films/films.php?id=6209.

Budansky, Stephen. "1620 to 1992: Long Ago but Not So Far Away (Imaginary Reaction of Boat People in 1620)." *U.S. News and World Report* 112, no. 22 (1992): 22.

Bybee, Roger, and Carolyn Winter. "Immigration Flood Unleashed by NAFTA's Disastrous Impact on Mexican Economy." April 25, 2006. www.commondreams.org/views06/0425-30.htm.

"Cable Act." Wikipedia. http://en.wikipedia.org/wiki/Cable_Act.

Calvin, John. *Commentary on the Prophet Isaiah*. Vol. 1. Grand Rapids, MI: Wm. B. Eerdmans, 1958.

Children's Immigration Advocate. "100,000-plus Citizen Children Find Parents Deported." March 15th, 2011. http://childrenimmigrationadvocate.com/03/100000-plus-citizen-children-find-parents-deported.

Church World Service. "Church World Service Resettles 5,322 Refugees in FY 2011 Toward 56,424 U.S. Refugee Program Total." October 14, 2011. www.churchworldservice.org/site/News2?page=NewsArticle&id=13211.

Coogan, Michael D., ed. *The New Oxford Annotated Bible*, 3rd edition, NRSV. New York: Oxford University Press, 2001.

Coombes, Andrea. "Hot Jobs for 2006: Services, Health Care." *York Sunday News* [York, PA], February 19, 2006.

Cose, Ellis. *A Nation of Strangers: Prejudice, Politics, and the Populating of America*. New York: William Morrow and Company, 1992.

Coudal, Mary Beth. "Humane Borders." Global Ministries. September 15, 2010. http://gbgm-umc.org/global_news/full_article.cfm?articleid=5846.

Daniel, Ben. *Neighbor: Christian Encounters with "Illegal" Immigration*. Louisville, KY: Westminster John Knox Press, 2010.

Dear, John. "Pharisee Nation: American Nation Brainwashed." CommonDreams.org, February 17, 2005. www.commondreams.org/views05/0215-21.htm.

Dharmaraj, Glory. "Human Trafficking Awareness and Action: A Bible Study." January 7, 2011. www.unitedmethodistwomen.org/resources/articles/item/index.cfm?id=355.

Digital History. "Landmarks in Immigration History." www.digital-history.uh.edu/historyonline/immigration_chron.cfm.

Dow, Mark. *American Gulag: Inside U.S. Immigration Prisons*. Berkeley: University of California Press, 2004.

Egan, Eileen. "Dorothy Day, Pilgrim of Peace." In *A Revolution of the Heart: Essays on the Catholic Worker*, edited by Patrick G. Coy. Philadelphia: Temple University Press, 1988.

Fix, Michael, and Jeffrey S. Passel. *Setting the Record Straight*. Washington, DC: Urban Institute, 1994.

Fluker, Walter Earl, and Catherine Tumer. *A Strange Freedom: The Best of Howard Thurman on Religious Experience and Public Life*. Boston: Beacon Press, 1998.

Franco, Jasmine. "*Jasmine's Story: ICE Teams apart Family*." General Board of Church and Society, August 6, 2010. www.umc-gbcs.org.

Free the Slaves. "About Slavery FAQ." www.freetheslaves.net/SSL-Page.aspx?pid=304.

Frelick, Bill. *U.S. Detention of Asylum Seekers and Human Rights*. Washington, DC: Migration Policy Institute, 2004.

Galedo, Lillian. "Dialogue & Initiative." *Immigration, Race, and Racism* (Winter 2003).

George, Sam. *Understanding the Coconut Generation: Ministry to the Americanized Asian Indians*. Niles, IL: Mall Publishing, 2006.

Gilbreath, Edward. *Reconciliation Blues: A Black Evangelical's Inside View of White Chrisitianity*. Nottingham, UK: IVP Books, 2006.

"Goals Set at 1993 Human Rights Conference Stymied by International Mistrust, India Tells Third Committee Review of Vienna Declaration and Action Plan." United Nations Press Release GA/SHC/3493, November 3, 1998. www.un.org/News/Press/docs/1998/19981103.gash3493.html.

Gonzalez, Eduardo, Jr. "Migrant Farmworkers: Our Nation's Invisible Population." May 27, 2008. www.extension.org/pages/9960/migrant-farm-workers:-our-nations-invisible-population.

Harding, Vincent. "Dangerous Spirituality." *Sojourners* (January–February 1999).

Herrick, Greg. "Paul and Civil Obedience in Romans 13:1–7." In *The Net Bible* (Richardson, TX: Biblical Studies Press, 1997). http://bible.org/article/paul-and-civil-obedience-romans-131-7.

Hershberger, Michelle. *A Christian View of Hospitality: Expecting Surprises.* Scottdale, PA: Herald Press, 1999.

Herzon, William R., II. *Parables as Subversive Speech: Jesus as Pedagogue of the Oppressed.* Louisville, KY: Westminster John Knox Press, 1994.

"History of Immigration to the United States." *Wikipedia,* http://en.wikipedia.org/wiki/Immigration_History_to_United_States.

Holthouse, David. "The Year in Hate." *Intelligence Report* (Spring 2009), www.splcenter.org/get-informed/intelligence-report/browse-all-issues/2009/spring/the-year-in-hate.

Homan, Daniel, and Lonni Collins Pratt. *Radical Hospitality: Benedict's Way of Love.* Brewster, MA: Paraclete Press, 2002.

"How to Challenge U.S. Immigrant Detention and Deportation Policies." April 19, 2011. www.unitedmethodistwomen.org/act/alerts/item/index.cfm?id=508.

Human Rights First. *In Liberty's Shadow: U.S. Detention of Asylum Seekers in the Era of Homeland Security.* New York: Human Rights First, 2004.

Human Rights Watch. *Detained and Dismissed: Women's Struggles to Obtain Health Care in United States Immigration Detention.* New York: Human Rights Watch, 2009.

Hunger Notes. "2011 World Hunger and Poverty Statistics: World Hunger Education Service." www.worldhunger.org/articles/Learn/world%20hunger%20facts%202002.htm.

Immigration Policy Center. "New Americans in the Great Lakes State." July 4, 2009. www.immigrationpolicy.org/just-facts/new-americans-great-lakes-state.

"Interfaith Statement in Support of Immigration Reform." October 24, 2008. www.interfaithimmigration.org/wp-content/up loads/2008/10/interfaith-cir-statement-final2.pdf.

Just Coffee. [Home page.] www.justcoffee.org.

Keefe, Patrick Radden. *The Snake Head: An Epic Tale of the Chinatown Underworld and the American Dream.* New York: Doubleday, 2009.

King, Martin Luther, Jr. "Address to First Mass Meeting Montgomery Improvement Association at Holt Street Baptist Church." December 5, 1955. http://mlk-kpp01.stanford.edu/index.php/encyclopedia/documentsentry/the_addres_to_the_first_montgomery_improvement_association_mia_mass_meeting.

King, Martin Luther, Jr. *Why We Can't Wait.* New York: Harper & Row, 1963.

Kirk, David. "Hospitality: Essence of Eastern Christian Lifestyle." *Diakonia* 16, no. 2 (1981): 104–117.

Kleist, James A. *The Didache: The Epistle to Diogenetus.* New York: Paulist Press, 1948.

Kochhar, Rakesh, Richard Fry, and Paul Taylor. "The Toll of the Great Recession: Hispanic Household Wealth Fell by 66% from 2005 to 2009." Pew Rearch Center, July 26, 2011. www.pewhis panic.org/2011/07/26/the-toll-of-the-great-recession.

Law, Eric H. F. *The Wolf Shall Dwell with the Lamb: A Spirituality for Leadership in a Multicultural Community.* St. Louis, MO: Chalice Press, 1993.

The Leadership Conference. "Confronting the New Faces of Hate: Hate Crimes in America 2009." www.civilrights.org/publications/hatecrimes/white-supremacist.html.

Loller, Travis. "Many Illegal Immigrants Pay Up at Tax Time." *USA Today*, April 4, 2008.

Lowell, B. Lindsey, Julia Gelatt, and Jeanne Batalova. *Immigrants and Labor Force Trends: The Future, Past, and Present*. Washington, DC: Migration Policy Institute, 2006.

Malik, Shiv. "UNHCR Report Says Refugee Numbers at 15-Year High." *The Guardian*, June 19, 2011.www.guardian.co.uk/world/2011/jun/20/unhcr-report-refugee-numbers-15-year-high.

Martin, Philip, and Elizabeth Midgley. "Immigration: Shaping and Reshaping America." *Population Bulletin* 58, no. 2 (June 2003).

"Mexico Mayor Killed as Tamaulipas Violence Escalates." BBC News, August 30, 2010. www.bbc.co.uk/news/world-latin-amer ica-11127005.

Migliore, Daniel L. *Faith Seeking Understanding: An Introduction to Christian Theology*. Grand Rapids, MI: Wm. B. Eerdmans, 1991.

Morrison, Toni. *Beloved*. New York: Penguin Books, 1987.

Mosala, I. J. *Biblical Hermeneutics and Black Theology in South Africa*. Grand Rapids, MI: Wm. B. Eerdsman, 1989.

"National Briefing, Southwest: New Mexico: A Mass for Border Crossers." *New York Times*, November 3, 2004. http://query.ny times.com/gst/fullpage.html?res=9C05E4DB163CF930A35752C 1A9629C8B63.

National Poverty Center. "Poverty in the United States: Frequently Asked Questions." www.npc.umich.edu/poverty.

"Native Americans of North America." Encarta Online Encyclopedia, 2005. http://encarta.msn.com.

Nettelhorst, R.P. "Notes on the Founding Fathers and the Separation of Church and State." October 2005. www.theology.edu/journal/volume2/ushistor.htm.

Nouwen, Henri, J. M. *The Only Necessary Thing: Living a Prayerful Life*. New York: The Crossroad Publishing Company, 1999.

Oduyoye, Mercy. *Hearing and Knowing: Theological Reflections on Christianity in Africa*. Maryknoll, NY: Orbis Books, 1986.

Office of Refugee Resettlement. "Unaccompanied Alien Children." Washington, DC: U.S. Department of Health and Human Services, 2006.

Passel, Jeffery S. and D'Vera Cohn. "U.S. Unauthorized Immigration Flows are Down Sharply Since Mid-Decade." Pew Research Center. September 1, 2010. http://pewhispanic.org/reports/report.php?ReportID=126.

PBS. "For Educators: Immigration Policy: Past and Present." www.pbs.org/independentlens/newamericans/foreducators_lesson_plan_03.html.

The Perryman Group. *An Essential Resource: An Analysis of the Economic Impact of Undocumented Workers on Business Activity in the U.S. with Estimated Effects by State and by Industry*. Houston, TX: Americans for Immigration Reform, 2008.

Peterson, Jim. "The Revolution of Belief." 2007. www.earlyamericanhistory.net/founding_fathers.htm.

Pohl, Christine D. *Making Room: Recovering Hospitality as a Christian Tradition*. Grand Rapids, MI: Wm. B. Eerdmans, 1999.

Quasten, Johannes, and Joseph C. Plumpe, eds. *Ancient Christian Writers: The Works of the Fathers in Translation.* New York: Paulist Press, 1948.

"Questioning Immigration Policy: Can We Afford to Open Our Arms?" Friends Committee on National Legislation Document #G-606-DOM, January 25, 1996.

Rah, Soong Chau. *The New Evangelism: Freeing the Church from Western Cultural Captivity.* Nottingham, UK: IVP Books, 2009.

Reed, Ishmael. *Mumbo Jumbo.* New York: Macmillian, 1972.

Refugees International. "Somalia." www.refintl.org/where-we-work/africa/somalia.

Refugees International. "Sudan." www.refintl.org/where-we-work/africa/sudan.

Rhodes, Stephen. *Where Nations Meet: The Church in a Multicultural World.* Nottingham, UK: IVP Books, 1998.

Robbins, Ted. "Nearly Half of Illegal Immigrants Overstay Visas." *All Things Considered,* June 14, 2006. www.npr.org/templates/story/story.php?storyId=5485917.

Social Principles of the United Methodist Church 2005–2008. Washington, DC: General Board of Church and Society of The United Methodist Church, 2005.

Soerens, Matthew, and Jenny Hwang. *Welcoming the Stranger: Justice, Compassion & Truth in the Immigration Debate.* Downers Grove, IL: IVP Books, 2009.

Terrazas, Aaron, and Cristina Batag. "Korean Immigrants in the United States." Migration Policy Institute. January 2009. www.migrationinformation.org/USfocus/display.cfm?ID=793.

Thurman, Howard. *Deep Is the Hunger*. Richmond, IN: Friends United Press, 1996.

Ufford-Chase, Rick. "Seeking God's Justice for People on the Move." *Church & Society Presbyterian Magazine* 95, no. 6 (2005): 5.

UNICEF Convention on the Rights of the Child. "Optional Protocol on the Sale of Children, Child Prostitution and Child Pornography." Updated June 2, 2011. www.unicef.org/crc/index_30204.html.

United Nations High Commissioner on Refugees. "Text of the 1951 Convention Relating to the Status of Refugees." www.unhcr.org/3b66c2aa10.html.

United Nations High Commission on Refugees. "UNHCR Urges More Countries to Establish Refugee Resettlement Programmes." July 5, 2010. www.unhcr.org/4c31cd236.html.

United Nations High Commission on Refugees. "Working with the Internally Displaced." www.unhcr.org/4ec230ebb.pdf.

United Nations High Commission on Refugees. "World Refugee Day: UNHCR Report Finds 80 Percent of World's Refugees in Developing Countries." June 20, 2011. www.unhcr.org/4dfb66ef9.html.

United Nations High Commission on Refugees Population and Geographical Data Section, Division of Operational Support. "Global Refugee Trends: Overview of Refugee Populations, New Arrivals, Durable Solutions, Asylum-Seekers, Stateless and Other Persons of Concern to UNHCR." Geneva: UNHCR. June 17, 2005.

U.S. Census Bureau. *American Community Survey: A Handbook for State and Local Officials*. Washington, DC: U.S. Department of Commerce, Economic & Statistics Administration, 2004.

U.S. Census Bureau. "American Fact Finder 2010: Selected Characteristics of the Total and Native Populations in the United States 2006–2010, American Community Survey 5-Year Estimates." http://Factfinder2.Census.Gov/Faces/Tableservices/Jsf/Pages/Productview.Xhtml?Pid=Acs_10_5yr_S0601&Prodtype=Table.

U.S. Commission on International Religious Freedom. "Annual Report 2011" (Washington, DC: USCIRF). www.uscirf.gov/images/book%20with%20cover%20for%20web.pdf.

U.S. Department of Homeland Security: U.S. Immigration and Customs Enforcement. *Detention Operations Manual*. Washington, DC: Bureau of Immigration and Customs Enforcement, 2004.

U.S. Department of State. "Trafficking in Persons Report 2010." www.state.gov/g/tip/rls/tiprpt/2010.

U.S. Department of State. "Visa Bulletin for June 2010." http://travel.state.gov/visa/bulletin/bulletin_4879.html.

U.S. Immigration and Naturalization Service. *INS Fact Book: Summary of Recent Immigration Data*. Washington, DC: Department of Justice, 1994.

Vanderpool, Tim. "Price of Admission." *Tucson Weekly*, June 5, 2008.

Weiner, Eric, and Lindsey Magnum. "Debunking Global Migration Myths." National Public Radio. June 6, 2007. www.npr.org/templates/story/story.php?storyId=10767136.

Wesley, John. "Explanatory Notes on the Whole Bible." www.biblestudytools.com/commentaries/wesleys-explanatory-notes.

Wesley, John. "John Wesley's Journals (Abridged)." www.revival-library.org/catalogues/1725ff/wesley.html.

Wesley, John. "Sermon on the Mount." In *The Works of John Wesley*. Vol. 1: *Sermons 1:1–33*, edited by Albert Outler. Nashville: Abingdon, 1984.

Wesley, John. "Thoughts Upon Slavery." General Board of Global Ministries, http://new.gbgm-umc.org/umhistory/wesley/slavery.

Who Is my Neighbor? Miami, FL: Church World Service and Christian Community Service Agency, 1995.

Wilkes, Sybella. *One Day We Had to Run.* Brookfield, CT: Millbrook Press, 1994.

Wolgin, Philip E., and Ann Garcia. "What Changes in Mexico Mean for U.S. Immigration Policy." The Center for American Progress. August 8, 2011. www.americanprogress.org/issues/2011/08/mexico_immigration.html.

World Bank. "Topics in Development: Migration & Remittances." July 2011. http://go.worldbank.org/RR8SDPEHO0.

World Watch Institute. "The State of Consumption Today." October 18, 2011. www.worldwatch.org/node/810.

World Watch Institute. *State of the World 2004: Richer, Fatter, and Not Much Happier.* New York: W. W. Norton, 2004.

Wood, Forrest G. *The Arrogance of Faith: Christianity and Racism in America.* New York: Alfred A. Knopf, 1991.

Wood, Gordon S. *The Radicalism of the American Revolution.* New York: Vintage Books, 1993.

Yancey, Phillip. *The Jesus I Never Knew.* Grand Rapids, MI: Zondervan, 1995.

Yong, Amos. *Hospitality and the Other: Pentecost, Christian Practices, and the Neighbor.* Maryknoll, NY: Orbis Books, 2008.

Young, Josiah Ulysses, III. *A Pan-African Theology: Providence and the Legacies of the Ancestors.* Trenton, NJ: African World Press, 1992.

Additional Resources

Campbell, Cynthia M. *A Multitude of Blessings: A Christian Approach to Religious Diversity.* Louisville: Westminster John Knox Press, 2007.
Although this book deals mainly with the issue of religious diversity, it has insights into the issues of the impact of language as well as the variety of religious practices and customs as they relate to the Church and the unity of the Body of Christ.

DeYoung, Curtiss Paul, Michael O. Emerson, George Yancey, and Karen Chai Kim. *United By Faith: The Multicultural Congregation as an Answer to the Problem of Race.* New York: Oxford University Press, 2003.
This book addresses multicultural congregations in the United States, but it has insights into the various ways cultures come together as one congregation from a historical as well as a practical view.

Foster, Charles R. *Leadership in Multicultural Congregations: Embracing Diversity.* Washington, DC: The Alban Institute, 1997.
This book deals with different congregations in the United States and the ways they employ to become inclusive.

Gebre-Selassie, Haileluel. *Integration Strategies of Migrant and Refugees.* London: Winston Churchill Memorial Trust of Australia, 2009. http://www.churchilltrust.com.au/site_media/fellows/Gebre-Selassie_Haileluel_2008.pdf.

This report compares the treatment of migrants and refugees in the United States, Germany, Canada, New Zealand, the United Kingdom, and Israel and makes recommendations for the Australian government in its development of national policies.

Green, Michael. *Evangelism in the Early Church*. Revised edition. Grand Rapids, MI: Wm. B. Eerdmans, 2003.
A classic dealing with the development of the early church and evangelism.

Grieco, Elizabeth. Defining *"Foreign Born" and "Foreigner" in International Statistics*. Washington, DC: Migration Policy Institute, 2008.
This publication helped to differentiate between the different types of understandings of citizenship—blood citizenship and birth citizenship.

Johnson, Alice. *Interpretation and Translation: Power Tools for Sharing Power in Grassroots Leadership Development*. Winston-Salem, NC: Mary Reynolds Babcock Foundation, 2002.
A publication of the study of translation and its effects on participation and leadership in El Centro Hispano.

Legrain, Philippe. *Immigrants: Your Country Needs Them*. London: Abacus, 2007.
This book develops a defense of migration and migration reform.

Oden, Amy G. *God's Welcome: Hospitality for a Gospel-Hungry World*. Cleveland: Pilgrim Press, 2008.
Great study book on hospitality using the biblical reflections, particularly the story of Abraham, on the four characteristics of radical hospitality: readiness, risk, repentance, and recognition.

Prill, Thorsten. *Global Mission on Our Doorstep: Forced Migration and the Future of the Church.* Muenster: MV Wissenschaft, 2008. This book offers several approaches to the church in the UK and its response to migration. The book focuses on the advantages and limits of the various approaches.

Smith, David I. *Learning from the Stranger: Christian Faith and Cultural Diversity.* Grand Rapids: Wm. B. Eerdmans, 2009. This book deals with the issues surrounding discipleship and cross-cultural issues. The author provides insight into superficial ways of connecting versus recognizing and loving strangers. He also addresses the issues surrounding using English as a common language.

Tira, Sadiri Joy, ed. *Scattered to Gather: Embracing the Global Trend of Dispora.* Manila: LifeChange Publishing, 2010. This report presents the concept and responsibilities of the Diaspora in the evangelizing of the world's global migrants.

Walls, Andrew, and Carol Ross, ed. *Mission in the 21st Century: Exploring the Five Marks of Mission.* Maryknoll, NY: Orbis Books, 2008. This book raises the issues facing the global church from the theoretical and practical standpoints. Essays explore the issues of mission and migration and worship and discipleship across cultures and the issue of differences in understanding the written word across culture and language.

Participant's Guide

This study guide is intended for individual readers who would like to augment their reading of the text by exploring further the issues discussed in the book and their feelings about them. Participating in this study guide will also help you prepare to be a contributing member of a larger study group. This guide is divided into four sections that focus on two chapters each and includes supplemental appendixes. Designate a notebook or journal in which to write down your answers to questions, participate in the activities, and journal about any feelings or insights you may have while reading the book and participating in the study guide.

Chapters 1 and 2

Then Jesus said to the Jews who had
believed in him, "If you continue in my word,
you are truly my disciples; and you will know
the truth, and the truth will make you free."

—John 8:31–32

Reading

"Then God said, 'Let us make humankind in our image, according to our likeness; and let them have dominion over the fish of the sea, and over the birds of the air, and over the cattle, and over all the wild animals of the earth, and over every creeping thing that creeps upon the earth.' So God created humankind in his image; male and female he created them" (Genesis 1: 26–27)

We the people of God are on a journey. It is a physical journey on earth as living images God, who said in Genesis 1:26, "Let us make humankind in our own image," and who also said in Matthew 25:40, "Just as you did it to one of the least of these who are members of my family, you did it to me." Wherever we are, whatever we are doing, and with whomever we are interacting, we must remember that we are each to the other, without exception, the image of God.

We also share a spiritual journey as we seek to live godly lives and plan and hope for life eternal with all God's people. Many of us see ourselves as strangers in this world on our way to eternal life in heaven. For this reason we identify with the strangers and include them in our journey. The stranger comes to teach us and give us a priceless gift—the gift of identity.

Prayer for Direction

Direct us, O Lord, in all our thoughts, our words, and our deeds. We come seeking to understand the role you would have us play in responding to strangers in our land. We come as followers of the refugee Christ, who at times had no place to lay his head. We come asking you to send the Holy Spirit to teach and guide us. We come, as followers of Christ, seeking to understand, to know, to accept, and to respond to the migrants, immigrants, refugees, and asylum seekers in our land. We come giving thanks for the food and security we celebrate in our lives. We seek to follow Christ's commandment of Love. Be with us we pray. Touch us. Teach us and guide us. Amen.

Study Questions

1. We have been created in the image of God and are on both a physical and spiritual journey. What role does the stranger in our midst play in that journey, and what role does God play in our individual migration stories?

2. Chapter 1 states that caring for the stranger is a vital part of our spiritual journey and that it is necessary to develop a new theology of radical, inclusive hospitality. How would you define this type of hospitality, and how would you compare and contrast it to the contemporary definition of hospitality?

3. What is the difference between biblical hospitality and contemporary hospitality?
4. Immigration is a hot-button topic for many people. Are we, as a nation, practicing a culture of hospitality toward immigrants or a culture of hostility toward immigrants? How are we acting as a church? As individuals?
5. As a people on a journey we do not travel alone. The text states, "A thorough study of scriptures makes it obvious that our journey is a communal migration story." What does this mean to you?

Activity

Draw a church and within it diagram the ethnic diversity of your church. Draw a picture of yourself and creatively diagram the ethnic diversity of your ancestral heritage and extended family.

Study Questions

1. The average person moves about twelve times in his or her life. Write down the number of times you have moved and why. What were your most common reasons for moving?
2. As a stranger in a new place, what did you most desire from your new community? Could this be a starting point for ministry to immigrants in your local area?
3. How do we live in a communal pattern with Christ at our center? How does this model reflect the Trinity?

Readings

Read the Prologue, Introduction, and Chapters 1 and 2.

Study Questions

1. Is it possible to go and sin no more?
2. What theme runs through scripture as a basis for eternal life?
3. Who has and who has not been created in God's image and as one of God's people? How does the answer impact a theology of radical, inclusive hospitality?
4. What is one way of explaining the teaching to deny ourselves and take up our cross?
5. How do we live out radical, inclusive theology and hospitality?
6. Do you identify yourself as a sinner or a saint? Explain.
7. In Luke 12:15 Jesus cautions, "Take care! Be on your guard against all kinds of greed; for one's life does not consist in the abundance of possessions." Does our nation's corporate and individual greed play into our attitudes toward strangers in our land?
8. What three groups does God identify for special care?
9. How does Jesus fit into the migration narrative? Where do you fit into the migration narrative?
10. What is the difference between seeing Christ in the stranger and Christ in you?
11. Martin Luther King Jr. wanted people to accept their redemptive role through embracing five objectives: self-respect, high moral standards, wholehearted work, leadership, and nonviolence. Would these five objectives work today in the establishment of a communal church that unites all believers in God's community and uplifts the unifying factors of diversity? If so, how might they be applied to the church?
12. We are all theologians. What steps might we take to

more closely follow the biblical mandate to welcome the stranger?

13. Margaret Mead is credited with saying, "Never doubt that a small group of thoughtful, committed citizens can change the world. Indeed it's the only thing that ever has." It is time for all people to claim their redemptive role by working to become an inclusive, hospitable community. What can we do to develop a radical, inclusive, hospitable community for all God's people?

14. What does it mean to live in community with Christ as the center, and how might that impact our ministries with immigrants?

Covenant

The conclusion of Chapter 1 begins by stating, "Jesus was the living proclamation of the Lord's favor. As his disciples we are called to live lives proclaiming the Lord's favor as well. As United Methodists, we are called to have open hearts, open minds, and open doors. Wherever we are, whatever we are doing, and with whomever we are interacting, we must remember that we are each to the other the image of God." Chapter 2 reminds us, "As disciples of Christ seeking to live lives of service and sacrifice, let us prayerfully consider offering hands of hope that create homes away from home to immigrants seeking new life, new acceptance, and a new place in God's all inclusive community."

As you begin this study on immigration and the Bible, think about how open your heart, mind, and doors are and those of your church, your family, your friends, and your community. There are many answers to this question. Covenant with yourself as you study this text to pray, "Change me, God. Change me according to your divine will."

Closing Prayer

In this time of learning and reflection, O God, open our hearts and minds to your presence. Send the Holy Spirit to touch us and teach us to more fully embrace the call Christ has on our lives. As we remember others who travel paths unknown to us, who speak other languages, and are in our land both with and without documents, fill us with your compassion. Enable us to see your face in the face of the stranger, and enable them to see your face and love in our faces. When our paths intersect, may we embrace one another with your love and continue our journey together by praying simply that you change us, God, change us that your will may be done in all things. Amen.

Homework

Choose to do one or both of the first or second assignments. The third should be done before you read Chapters 3 and 4.

1. Using art, poetry, prose, music, lyrics, dance, drama, or any other creative medium, create a product that compares or contrasts your migration story to some segment of the biblical migration story.
2. Make a collage or chart of your family's immigration story using actual pictures of your family members or photos or pictures that represent your family's ancestry.
3. Read Appendix 1 on definitions of key terms relating to this study on immigration and familiarize yourself with these terms.
4. Read Chapters 3 and 4 of the text.

Chapters 3 and 4

Go from your country and your kindred and your
father's house to the land that I will show you.

—Genesis 12:1

Reading
Psalm 137 (adapted): By the Waters of the Rio Grande

By the waters of the Rio Grande, there we sat down and there
we wept when we remembered Zion. On the willows there we
hung up our guitars, for there the border patrol asked us for
songs and the vigilantes asked for laughter, saying, "Sing us one
of the songs of Zion!" How could we sing the Lord's song in
a foreign land? By the waters we weep and we remember. We
remember Mexico and El Salvador. We remember Honduras
and Darfur. We remember Colombia and Bosnia. We remember Cuba and Haiti. We remember China and Romania. By the
waters we remember. On the willows we hung up our guitars.
We hung up our hopes. We hung up our homes, our land, our
dreams. We hung up our poverty, our hunger, our thirst. We
hung up our friends, our traditions our culture. We hung up our
family ties, our food, our language. How shall we sing the Lord's
song in a foreign land? We sing only the song of the homeless,
the unemployed, the laments of hunger and thirst, of death and

destruction, the songs of the songless, the hungry, the thirsty, the songs of the lonely, the songs of the dying. How shall we sing the Lord's song in a foreign land?

Prayer for Direction

God of refuge, you have been with our ancestors as they traveled to this land to build a new life. Through them, we have found our home here and in you. Help us to open ourselves to the strangers among us: the immigrants, the refugees, the migrants, and the asylum seekers. Help us to be truly grateful that our physical needs are met and be willing to share with those in need. Open our hearts and minds as we seek your will in responding to the strangers in this land, and remind us that once we too were strangers in this land. Change us, O God. Please change us according to your will. Amen.

Study Questions

1. How do you understand the concept that God migrates with the people?
2. What are the three groups in the Hebrew Bible that are repeatedly named as recipients of biblical hospitality?
3. What is the biblical mandate found in both the Hebrew Bible and the New Testament on welcoming the stranger?
4. How are you and/or your church community responding to that mandate?
5. How might you more fully respond?

Activity

Make a list of changes in the church since 1950. Make a list of changes in the home since 1950. Compare the lists. Which area has the most changes and why? Compile a list on the ways other cultures are reflected in your church and spiritual life. Compile another list of the way other cultures are reflected in your day-to-day life and home, work, and play. Analyze the reasons for the differences.

Study Questions

1. What would it mean to be a church offering radical, inclusive hospitality?
2. Why does there seem to be a desire to keep the church the way it is? Is there this same desire to keep the rest of our lives the way they are? Why the difference in perspectives?
3. According to the teachings of Jesus, how are we to respond to violence?
4. Do you know any Muslims? People of other faiths? Please list them and briefly state what you know about their beliefs.
5. Do you have in mind a picture of a Muslim? Hagar had a son to Abraham, as did Sarah. As Abraham's child, if you were drawing a family tree, what would your relationship be to Ishmael and to Isaac?

Activity

How does being created in the image of God impact your ministry and life? Diagram, draw, write, or create a presentation about your being created in the image of God.

Reading

Read "Maria's Story." (See Appendix 2.) Following the story, journal some of your feelings and opinions.

Closing Prayer

Creator God, across the ages you have blessed and protected people on the move. We come to you seeking guidance as we explore scripture and seek to welcome sisters and brothers from across the globe. Help us to open our hearts, minds, homes, and churches to strangers in our communities. Remind us that just as Christ welcomed everyone he met, we are to do likewise. Please give wisdom and courage to those who make and enforce immigration laws. Be with us as we continue to study immigration issues and change us, we pray. Change us that your will be done as we seek to offer radical inclusive hospitality to whomever you bring into our lives. Amen.

Homework

Read Chapters 5 and 6. Decide whom you most identify with and (1) journal what action you feel Christ would call for in response to the situation presented or (2) write your own psalm or rewrite one of the Psalms to reflect a contemporary immigration story or viewpoint.

Chapters 5 and 6

Do not press me to leave you or to turn back from
following you! Where you go, I will go; where you
lodge, I will lodge; your people shall be my people,
and your God my God.

—Ruth 1:16

Reading

Many migrants leave their loved ones to seek employment and send money (known as remittances) home to support their families. Some of us wonder how anyone can leave his or her children and migrate to another land for work. In our culture, it is almost unthinkable, but if we were living in rural poverty in a developing country and making one dollar a day (or less), we would begin to understand the drive to migrate. Moving to the nearest developed country would make a great deal of sense. The options are to migrate or watch children and loved ones starve.

In Haiti and other very poor countries, it is not uncommon for a mother to have to decide which child she feeds and which child she lets starve. During 2011, as famine spread over the Horn of Africa, we watched story after story of families walking for days to a refugee camp seeking medical aid and food. National news showed us a mother with a two-year-old child who weighed seven pounds and others carrying emaciated children who were dying in their arms. Stories were told of leaving children and family members to die under trees or shrubs as the family moved on to seek help for the living. Migrants walk for food, for life, for work, and in hope of finding radical, inclusive, hospitable people who will recognize their humanity and give them a chance at new life.

Deuteronomy 24:19–21 instructs us,

> When you reap your harvest in your field and forget a sheaf in the field, you shall not go back to get it; it shall be left for the alien, the orphan, and the widow, so that the Lord your God may bless you in all your undertakings. When you beat your olive trees, do not strip what is left; it shall be for the alien, the orphan, and the widow. When you gather the grapes of your vineyard, do not glean what is left; it shall be for the alien, the orphan, and the widow. Remember that you were a slave in the land of Egypt; therefore I am commanding you to do this.

Prayer for Direction

God of refuge, you have traveled with us throughout the ages. You are walking with us in our darkest moments and crying with the trafficked, enslaved, oppressed, and marginalized. We come to you today asking that you change and open our hearts, our minds, and our doors to sisters and brothers who throughout the ages have been victimized. We give you thanks for scriptures that guide us and for Christ who came to us as a migrant and refugee and offered us salvation. We give you thanks for the Holy Spirit who moves with us as we migrate physically, emotionally, and intellectually to new lands that you have prepared for us. As we continue this study, we ask that you change us according to your divine will to be the hands and feet of Christ in our world as we seek to offer hospitality to strangers, remembering that to them we are the stranger. Change us, O Lord. Change us, we pray. Amen.

Thought

How has the use of the prayer asking God to change you impacted you? Have you noticed any changes in thoughts, feelings, actions, attitudes, desires, etc.?

Study Questions

1. Consider the stories of Ruth and Naomi (from the book of Ruth). Are similar situations happening today? Explain and describe.

2. How would you differentiate between Ruth's actions that result in her marriage to Boaz and those of a modern-day migrant who seeks a partner to bring stability to her life?

3. How would migrants be treated in the United States if we followed the Hebrew Bible teachings of Ruth and Deuteronomy?

4. Do you think it is fair to refuse to legalize a spouse of a U.S. citizen because that person came into the country without documents?

5. In the book of Esther, Esther was told perhaps she was married to the King for "such a time as this." Her presence resulted in a greater good for her people. Do you believe God places us in situations for "such a time as this?" If so, give examples. (Please keep in mind that "such a time as this" may be an interaction with

a much smaller part of God's creation than Esther impacted.)

6. Where have you been placed by God and what are you called to do?
7. Is it true that everyone wants to come to the United States? Explain your answer.
8. Do you know of any trafficking situations in your town, state, or country? Describe them.
9. Have you ever fasted? In Isaiah 58:6–10, God speaks about the desired type of fasting. How could it be incorporated into your personal and corporate faith practices?
10. Do you agree that there is a Christian myth of superiority?
11. Keeping in mind that many undocumented persons are living in indentured servitude or worse, how did and do Christians justify slavery and indentured servitude?

Activity

Begin to create or plan a work that shows how your life is tied up in a global identity. Draw or write or create a collage of your identity, listing languages, customs, traditions, pastimes, food, music, styles, décor, and dress that are important to you and as many ethnic groups you touch or who touch you that make you who you are today.

Study Questions

1. Immigration is a hot button issue for many of us—our friends, our families, our church, and our communities. Why?
2. What is the advice given by the Hebrew Bible on how we should respond to immigrants in the land?

Activity
Consider the idea of developing a prayer ministry using the seniors and persons who are physically disabled to undergird and support the ministries of the church and the needs of the people of your community, including documented and undocumented immigrants. Come up with ways people with opposing viewpoints can pray in one accord on any topic. Give the ministry a name and a focus and explain how you would go about developing this ministry.

Reading
"Welcoming the Strangers—Refugees, Migrants, Asylum Seekers." (See Appendix 3.)

Closing Prayer
Creed for Immigrants

We believe in almighty God, who guided God's people in exile and in exodus, the God of Joseph in Egypt and of Daniel in Babylon, the God of foreigners and immigrants. We believe in Jesus Christ a displaced Galilean, who was born away from his people and his home, who had to flee the country with his parents when his life was in danger, and who upon returning to his own country had to suffer the oppression of the tyrant Pontius Pilate, the servant of a foreign power. He was persecuted, beaten, tortured, and finally accused and condemned to death unjustly. But on the third day, this scorned Jesus rose from the dead, not as a foreigner but to offer us citizenship in heaven.

We believe in the Holy Spirit, the eternal immigrant from God's Kin-dom among us, who speaks all languages, lives in all countries, and reunites all races. We believe that the church is the secure home for all foreigners and believers who constitute it; it speaks the same language and has the same purpose. We believe that the communion of saints begins when we accept the diversity of the saints. We believe in forgiveness, which makes us all equal, and in reconciliation, which identifies us more than does race, language or nationality. We believe that in the Resurrection, God will unite us as one people in which all are distinct and all are alike at the same time. We believe in the eternal life beyond this world, where no one will be an immigrant but all will be citizens of God's Kin-dom that has no end. Amen.

Homework
Read Chapters 7 and 8.

Chapters 7 and 8

Do not neglect to show hospitality to strangers,
for by doing that, some have entertained angels
without knowing it. Remember those who are in
prison, as though you were in prison with them;
those who are being tortured, as though you
yourselves were being tortured.

—Hebrews 13:2–4

Reading
"Jasmine's Story" (See Appendix 4.)

Prayer for Direction
Open our eyes that they may see the deepest needs of men and women. Move our hands that they may feed the hungry. Touch our heart that it may bring warmth to the despairing. Teach us generosity that welcomes strangers. Let us share our possessions to clothe the naked. Give us the care that strengthens the sick. Make us share in the quest to set the prisoners free. In sharing our anxiety and our love, our poverty, and our prosperity, we partake of your divine presence. Amen. (Source: Canaan Banana, Zimbabwe. *With All God's People: The New Ecumenical Prayer Cycle* [Geneva: WCC Publications, 1989], 344).

Study Questions

1. How is the Trinity an example of inclusivity?
2. How do communities model a triune relationship?
3. How can we build radical, inclusive, hospitable communities?
4. How does communion make us blood relatives?
5. What is God's mandate in the Hebrew Bible and how would Christ ask us to respond?
6. How would imagining Jesus as Love rather than Lord affect your relationships?
7. David Kirk said, "Hospitality becomes for the Christian community a way of being the sacrament of God's love in the world."* Do you agree? Please explain.

Activity

Jasmine's story happens hundreds or perhaps thousands of times each week in the United States and around the world. Write a letter to a child whose mother has been deported and explain why it had to happen, how you feel about it, and your hopes and prayers for the coming years, or write a letter to an immigration detainee who has never committed a crime but is detained because her work visa expired and she remained in the United States in order to send money home to feed her family.

Study Questions

1. What are your feelings about families being separated because of immigration status?
2. What steps can a church take to develop a program of radical, inclusive hospitality toward immigrants?

---

*David Kirk, "Hospitality: Essence of Eastern Christian Lifestyle," *Diakonia* 16, no. 2 (1981): 112.

3. Does your church host a Justice for Our Neighbors ministry? If not, do you feel this would be a good ministry for your local church and why?
4. What types of ministries with uprooted people could local churches develop?

Reading

Galatians 3:28 states, "There is no longer Jew or Greek; there is no longer slave or free; there is no longer male or female; for all of you are one in Christ Jesus." Until we are all—each and everyone of us—free to be exactly the person God has created us to be, none of us are free. As long as there is one person who cannot walk the streets with his or her head held high and feel the sunshine on his or her face, none of us can truly walk with our heads held high.

Study Questions

1. Is becoming politically active a way to "get our hands dirty"? Where does social and political activism fit into the concept of radical, inclusive hospitality?
2. United Methodist Women members have identified detention of immigrants as a key area of concern and have become advocates for detention reform. What are their key areas of concern on this issue?
3. Do you believe we are called as followers of Christ to advocate for immigration reform and reform of the detention of immigrants? Explain your answer.
4. Brainstorm ways to become an immigration advocate.

Activity

In no more than two sentences for each, respond to the following questions taking both sides of the issue (for example, two sentences explaining why God's authority is primary and two sentences explaining why human's authority is primary, etc.): Whose authority is primary? God's or human's? How does your answer impact your life? Do you believe all authority comes from God? Why or why not? Which do you follow the most? God's law or human's law? Eugene Peterson writes in *The Message* that "all governments are under God. Insofar as there is peace and order. It's God's order." Do you agree? Are all laws good laws? Is there a responsibility to speak out if human's laws are in opposition to God's laws? If so, how is that to be done?

Study Questions

1. What generalizations can you make about the history of U.S. immigration law?
2. Have the laws been written to favor one or more particular groups?
3. How have the laws changed over the past fifty years?
4. What laws are surprising to you?
5. What is the difference between an immigration detainee and an inmate in a regular prison or jail?
6. Do the immigration laws follow God's laws? Explain.
7. If you could write one new immigration law, what would it be?

Reading

The Good Samaritan and the Strangers

A small country was caught between an extended war between two powerful countries. The citizens of the country were divided in their support of the warring nations. When one country withdrew, their supporters were targeted for persecution and imprisonment by the supporters of the victorious government. Many feared that they might be killed. Their homes were destroyed, family members were mistreated, and many lost their jobs.

Although they loved their homeland, they had no choice but to flee for their safety. Some could prove they were political, social, or religious refugees. Others were considered economic migrants and unwelcomed in the country to which they fled. They were undocumented.

The governor of one country said they were taking the jobs of its citizens and collecting welfare (even though it was impossible to get welfare without documents). The legislators passed laws to have everyone without documents deported. They even insisted that the schools report any children who might have undocumented parents. Another governor saw what was happening and took time to study the issue, saying, "We'll help, even though we have similar problems."

This country had faith-based organizations that assisted immigrants, migrants, refugees, and asylum seekers. These organizations began asking their members to demonstrate their faith by sponsoring refugees, providing legal clinics for immigrants, opening migrant welcome centers, advocating for immigration reform and legalization, and building radical, hospitable, faith-based communities.

A very large, beautiful, financially secure church with a large congregation and many programs for its members was asked to help. They responded, "Oh, we're too busy getting ready for our one hundredth anniversary. Maybe next year we'll think about it if there are still refugees." But a very small congregation struggling to keep itself financially stable heard about the need for refugee housing and offered to help, and some other congregations quickly offered assistance. One of these congregations didn't even have their own building, another had just completed a building project, and another had just raised money for a major denominational appeal, but they said they would do whatever was necessary to help.

Which of these governors and congregations proved to be a neighbor to these families? (Source: Adapted from an original version by Quentin Goodrich based on Luke 10:25–37, published in the newsletter of the Florida Council of Churches, March 1981.)

Closing Prayer

We go now as sojourners in the land, pilgrims passing through. We go to accept responsibility for the land we are passing through. We know that we are the voice of the voiceless and the hands and feet of Christ our Lord. The community of God is neither here nor there. The community of God is among us. We go with God, walk with Christ, and are open to the guidance of the Holy Spirit. We welcome the strangers in our midst. Amen.

Appendix 1: Terms Defined

alien: A person who is not a citizen of the country in which he or she lives.

asylee: A person who has been granted permission to stay in a country of which he or she is not a citizen.

asylum seeker: A person seeking safety in another country from persecution at home. Asylum is based on a well-founded fear of persecution for reasons of race, religion, nationality, membership in a particular social group, or political opinion.

Border Patrol: A branch of the U.S. Department of Homeland Security that polices the borders of the United States. It is concentrated on the border between the United States and Mexico and the United States and Canada and seeks to prevent persons from entering the United States without proper immigration papers.

DHS: U.S. Department of Homeland Security, which is in charge of national security, including immigration.

exile: To banish a person from his or her country or home.

expedited removal: To send people back to their country of origin before admitting them to the country to which they have fled. Officials at U.S. airports may "refuse entry" to a person without giving him or her the opportunity to make a claim for asylum before an immigration judge.

forced migrant: A person forced to leave his or her country or home to seek safety, shelter, and sustenance.

guest worker: A worker in a country with an immigration visa granting permission to work and live in the country for a period of time.

immigrant: A person who settles in a country of which he or she is not a native.

migrant: A person who leaves a place to seek safety, shelter, and sustenance, which includes employment.

refugee: A person fleeing his or her country because of a well-founded fear of persecution for reasons of race, religion, nationality, membership in a particular social group, or political opinion.

repatriate: To return a person to his or her country either with the person's consent or forcibly.

resettlement: Moving from a first country of asylum to a second country for permanent relocation when there is no hope of returning home. A person who has resettled in a second country is not eligible for asylum from the first country.

sanctuary: A safe place offering refuge.

trafficking: Smuggling human beings from one country to another, often for illegal purposes, such as indentured servitude or sexual slavery.

unaccompanied alien minor: A child under eighteen years of age who enters a country alone or is trafficked into the country. If apprehended, the unaccompanied minor may be detained in federal detention centers before being returned to the home country or being released to a relative or friend.

undocumented: A person who enters a country without papers.

uprooted: Condition of being forced to leave home for environmental, political, religious, ethnic, social, or economic reasons.

Appendix 2: Maria's Story

This was written by the Rev. Barb Dinnen of Las Americas Faith Community, Trinity United Methodist Church in Des Moines, Iowa, June 2009. Used with permission.

Maria died on a Monday night, but the coroner didn't register her death officially until Tuesday morning. He said the official cause of death was exposure, meaning exposure to the heat and cold, sun and drought of the dessert that she crossed from Mexico to Arizona. I guess I would say she died of exposure not only to the cruel elements of nature but to cruel, unjust immigration laws, to cold hearts and hot tempers driven by fear of the privileged population believing the "Marias" of the world want to "take from" them.

"Take what?" I wonder. Would they take anything nearly as valuable as your family, the ones you love, the very heart of your being? Maria knew what it was like to be separated from her family. When her mother had fled to the United States from El Salvador during the war years with the hope of finding a job so she could send money back to feed the family, Maria stayed in Usulutan, El Salvador, to take care of her grandmother. Maria's brothers came to the United States at different times for different reasons. When abuelita died, it was Maria's time to finally reunite with her mother who by that time was a permanent resident.

When Maria crossed the border she was stopped by Immigration and Customs Enforcement (ICE) officials and was given a court date to appear before a judge in Texas. Her family paid the required fees and brought Maria to Iowa. Because Texas was far away and Maria did not have a lawyer to ask how to change the venue, she didn't appear before a judge, which was an automatic cause for the judge to issue a deportation order.

Around nine years later at seven o'clock in the morning, ICE officials knocked on her mother's door. Maria, always cheerful and friendly, opened the door and they barged into the house. They had a piece of paper with someone's name and picture on it. The family knew the name, but the person had never lived in that house and they thought he moved out of state. The ICE agents asked for everyone to show their IDs and then they arrested Maria, her brother, and a family friend. Her brother was released on bond, but Maria was deported in April.

From El Salvador, Maria told her mother she was coming back to the United States. Her mother begged her not to, but Maria made arrangements with a coyote and paid him $6,500, which provided her a trip and guide through Mexico, mostly in taxis or vans, and then another guide would take her over the border. The group of twenty-one prepared to walk two nights, all night long. They made it through the first night, but during the second night they were spotted by a helicopter and they hid. Later the helicopter came back and sent agents to capture them. Half of the group was caught, but Maria was one of a small group that followed the coyote and escaped. They regrouped and decided they would wait a day and go another way.

On the day they were to take off, Maria called her mom and told her the story—her fear, the exhaustion, the thirst, the hunger, the bruises and bumps. Her mother heard Maria's deep, profound cough and begged her daughter to turn back, but she did not. As they walked they heard the helicopter overhead and they all dove into the hot, biting sand. The helicopters flew away. Before the day was up Maria became weak. A friend carried Maria in his arms because she could no longer walk. The rest of the group was impatient with him. That evening he knew that she had died. The others in the group said, "Put her down. She's already dead. Put her down so we can get going!"

"No!" he cried. "She is a human being, not an animal. I'm not leaving her here!"

The others took off without them. Maria's friend found shade under a tree, put her under the tree, and covered her with a sweater. He walked for two hours trying to find someone to help, anyone, with no luck. He returned to Maria and carried her to the highway, which took the rest of the night. Early in the morning he reached the highway and set her body along the side of the road and went in search of anyone who could help him. He found an immigration station and told them where he had left the body and how they could identify her. His arms were bloody and bruised from carrying Maria through the night. He was exhausted and weak from hunger and thirst. Immigration officials put handcuffs around his bloody wrists and arrested him. After he was processed, he was allowed to call Maria's family to explain what had happened. They say they will always be grateful for her friend's compassion and sacrifice. If he hadn't made such a sacrifice, Maria's body would have been left along the way, unidentifiable, unburied, abandoned to the forces of nature.

Maria's friend feels fortunate. Normally a person caught while returning to the United States after he or she has been deported receives an automatic long-term jail sentence. His lawyers have given him hope that he will be in jail for only a couple of months before they deport him. Because of his heroic and humanitarian efforts, the lawyer hopes they will be lenient with him.

Maria's family knows many, many people who have crossed as Maria did, and they have heard of the hundreds of people who die each year, but they never knew anyone who had died. They were sure it had to be a mistake until they actually saw her body. They couldn't imagine another option except to have her body brought to Iowa; however, they had no idea that the complete cost of the sending and preparing the body and the coffin and burial plot would cost seventeen thousand dollars. They would have done the same had they known ahead of time, but they continue wondering if there would have been a cheaper way.

Appendix 3: Welcoming the Strangers — Refugees, Migrants, Asylum Seekers

A Message on Welcoming the Stranger and Scriptural Conflict: Governing Authority or God's Authority?

Refugees are people who have been forced to cross international borders because they fear being persecuted because of their race, ethnicity, religion, membership in a particular social group, or political affiliation. In the United States, refugees must be identified as refugees in a country other than their country of origin and then interviewed and cleared for admission to the U.S. resettlement program. Less than 1 percent of the world's refugees are ever permanently resettled. An asylum seeker fears the same type of persecution as refugees but asks for asylum on arriving in a safe country. Migrants are forced to leave their homes seeking gainful employment to support their families or themselves. The following message, a worship service, demonstrates how our biblical ancestors would be welcome under current immigration law.

SOLO: "By the Babylonian Rivers" (*The Faith We Sing*, no. 2217)

FIRST READER: Romans 13:1–5
Let every person be subject to the governing authorities; for there is no authority except from God, and those authorities that exist have been instituted by God. Therefore whoever resists authority resists what God has appointed, and those who

resist will incur judgment. For rulers are not a terror to good conduct, but to bad. Do you wish to have no fear of the authority? Then do what is good, and you will receive its approval; for it is God's servant for your good. But if you do what is wrong, you should be afraid, for the authority does not bear the sword in vain! It is the servant of God to execute wrath on the wrongdoer. Therefore one must be subject, not only because of wrath but also because of conscience.

ADAM: Our names are Adam and Eve. We disobeyed our Creator and were sent into exile to till and live off the land.

EVE: We can't go home. Will you welcome us?

CONGREGATION: Do you have documents giving you permission to be here? The United States welcomes only persons with proper travel documents. If you don't have permission to be here, we cannot welcome you. We are sorry but you must go.

NOAH: My name is Noah. There was a great flood! Only my family and the animals—two of each kind—survived. Our home is gone. Please take us in.

CONGREGATION: Natural disasters need to be dealt with where they happened. We can't take everyone in. You are migrants. Sorry, go somewhere else. Our laws do not provide a place for you.

ABRAHAM: God told us to leave our homes and to travel to this the place God has shown us.

SARAH: Will you give us a home?

CONGREGATION: People who hear voices are not wanted here. You would drain our medical system. We would have to pay for your health care. Sorry, the United States is selective about who can come to our country.

JACOB: I am Jacob. My older brother has threatened to kill me. I can't go home. Please take me in.

CONGREGATION: We have our own family problems. Domestic violence is not grounds for admittance. Our laws will not grant you sanctuary. Sorry, go home and work it out with your brother.

JOSEPH: I am Joseph. My brothers sold me into slavery. I was brought to the United States to work. Please help me.

CONGREGATION: Slavery is against the law. We don't have slaves in the United States. You must have the proper documents to work here. You have no legal right to be here. Sorry, you will be sent home.

JOSEPH'S BROTHERS: We are Joseph's brothers. There is famine in our land. We have no food to eat. Will you feed us and give us a home?

CONGREGATION: Famine and starvation are not grounds for admission to the United States. You would eat our food and take our jobs. Sorry, our county's laws will not let you stay here. You must return to your home country and see if you can find a legal way to get here.

MOSES: My name is Moses. I killed an Egyptian who was mistreating my people. I had to flee. Please, please protect me.

CONGREGATION: You are a criminal alien. There are laws against people like you. The United States doesn't give asylum to criminals. Sorry, you will be sent back. We have enough of our own criminals.

AARON: I am Aaron, spokesperson for the nation of Israel. We are workers, good brickmakers, carpenters, and farmworkers. We are strong and willing workers. We are looking for the Promised Land. We are seeking permission to enter. My people are waiting on the other side of the fence, and we can harvest your crops and build your houses.

CONGREGATION: You are migrants! You had jobs in your country; you just didn't like the working conditions and you think you can get better pay here. Sorry, we need our jobs for our people. You are undocumented. You will have to stay on the other side of the border.

RUTH: I am Ruth. My husband died, and I followed my mother-in-law to her country, the United States. Naomi is my only family. Please help me.

CONGREGATION: Naomi is welcome. She is a citizen, but you have no legal right to be here—you are not her daughter. We are sorry that your husband died, but you will have to leave. We don't want you harvesting our crops and taking our benefits.

ESTHER: I am Esther. I have been trafficked and was brought here to be used for a high official's sexual pleasure. Please help me.

CONGREGATION: You have no right to be here. Trafficked people are not allowed in this country. We are a moral people who are subject to the governing authorities. They will put you in prison until we can deport you. You weren't persecuted—you were just kidnapped. Your country should protect you. Sorry, but you will have to go home.

JOSEPH: I am Joseph. This is my wife, Mary, and our son, Jesus. We have had to flee our country because the king is killing all the boys under two years of age.

MARY: We fled in the middle of the night. We have nothing, and we have no identification. Will you give us work and sanctuary and asylum?

CONGREGATION: We are willing to help you, but there are laws that have to be followed. Our law states that if you enter without documents, you have to seek asylum from prison. Joseph, you will go to one prison. Mary, you will go to another, and Jesus, you will go to a third (until we find foster care for you, that is). We are sorry, but that's the law.

SAMARITAN: Please help me. I'm from Samaria and I'm not documented. I saw a man, a United States citizen, being robbed. I stopped to help him. The police came, and when they asked for identification, I ran. I just tried to help. Please help me. My wife is a U.S. citizen and our children will starve if I can't work.

CONGREGATION: Laws have to be followed. You have no right to be here. Our government will send you back. We are sorry, but you will have to leave the United States. Since your wife is a U.S. citizen, she and the children can stay here without you or leave and go with you.

JESUS: They call me Jesus. I come begging for help for my twelve friends. When we got off the plane, we asked for asylum. My friends were being persecuted in our homeland for following me. But the U.S. government officials didn't believe us. Everyone but me is in expedited removal; they are all being sent back. I managed to slip away and came here to this church to ask for help.

CONGREGATION: The United States has laws to keep out terrorists. You are one of a group of thirteen Middle Eastern men we've heard about. You meet in rented rooms, you go into the mountains for private meetings, no one knows where you get your money, and you travel by boat and meet with strangers. You are trying to organize the poor and the oppressed. You could very well be a terrorist. Expedited removal will make certain you can't harm us. We are sorry, but you and the twelve other men will have to leave. It's the law.

SECOND READER: Romans 12:9–13
Let love be genuine; hate what is evil, hold fast to what is good; love one another with mutual affection; outdo one another in showing honor. Do not lag in zeal, be ardent in spirit, serve the Lord. Rejoice in hope, be patient in suffering, persevere in prayer. Contribute to the needs of the saints; extend hospitality to strangers.

THIRD READER: Romans 13:8
Owe no one anything, except to love one another; for the one who loves another has fulfilled the law.

JESUS: Come, you that are blessed by my Father, inherit the kingdom prepared for you from the foundation of the world; for I was hungry and you gave me food, I was thirsty and you gave me something to drink, I was a stranger and you welcomed me, I was naked and you gave me clothing, I was sick and you took care of me, I was in prison and you visited me. Then the righteous will answer him, "Lord, when was it that we saw you hungry and gave you food, or thirsty and gave you something to drink? And when was it that we saw you a stranger and welcomed you, or naked and gave you clothing? And when was it that we saw you sick or in prison and visited you?" And the king will answer them, "Truly I tell you, just as you did it to one of the least of these who are members of my family, you did it to me." (Matthew 25:34–40)

Closing Prayer

God of immigrants and refugees, you have saved us from all that has threatened us since the beginning of our days. We are strangers who have found our home in you. Help us to open our hearts and hands to those who come seeking freedom and life. Save them as we strive to be their sanctuary. We pray in the name of our refugee brother, Jesus the Christ. Amen.

Closing Song

"Sanctuary" (*The Faith We Sing*, no. 2164)

Appendix 4: Jasmine's Story

From "Jasmine's Story: ICE Tears apart Family" by Jasmine Franco for the General Board of Church and Society, August 6, 2010 (www.umc-gbcs.org). Reprinted with permission.

My name is Jasmine Franco. I am 18 years old. I was born in Chicago, but my parents are from Guatemala. This summer I graduated from Huron High School in Ann Arbor, Michigan. I felt very proud of myself for graduating because I am the first person in my immediate family to graduate from high school. And when I start at Washtenaw Community College in the fall, I will be the first in my family to attend college.

Before I get into more, I want to ask you a question: How would you feel if you were separated from your family and forced to live by yourself? And how would you feel if at age seventeen you had to support yourself? This happened to me.

On November 22, 2008, my family was going out to eat at my mother's favorite restaurant, La Fuente in Ypsilanti. We were heading out when Immigration and Customs Enforcement (ICE) agents pushed our front door open. They came into our house without asking permission. They yelled at us to get down on the floor. When they saw my mother, they searched her and then told us to sit down.

They showed us their badges that said ICE. As soon as I saw the word ICE I started crying. I knew what was going to happen to my mother. The agents asked my mother for her papers, but she was terrified and confused. She didn't know what to say to them. So she ran to the room and got the papers of my twelve-year-old sister, Jennifer, and me, hoping they would feel sorry for her and let her go. The agents were not sorry for anyone, though. My mother had been in the United States for nineteen years. She is a hardworking woman and the best mother. Unfortunately, I am now away from her.

I used to visit her every Thursday at the Calhoun County Jail's immigration holding facilities. While she was there, my mother lost so much weight. Almost every day she found flies in her food and wouldn't eat it. My father would give me money to put in her account so she could order food that was sealed, such as soups and chips.

My mother also faced discrimination by a jailer. It got to the point that when we sent my mother photos the jailer ripped them off the walls and cut them up in my mother's face. The jailer would throw them on the floor and then tell my mother to pick them up. My mother was really upset.

My mother is now in Guatemala, away from me, because she got deported. She was deported on January 21, 2009, the day after my birthday. I couldn't even say good-bye to her and give her a hug.

I still had my father and sister until February 2, 2009. My father was certain he would get caught too. So he decided to leave. I went with him to the airport. It was really sad watching him and my sister go away, knowing that we most likely will never be together again.

My dad was really sad, torn apart that he had to leave his seventeen-year-old daughter in this country by herself. He did not want to go and leave me. I can still remember him walking, looking back every twenty seconds or so. I couldn't stop crying. It was the worst moment in my life: now I had just lost my father and sister, too.

After my dad left I had to live by myself. I went to school and worked at my mother's former job for a cleaning company. It was very difficult. I got home from work around 11:30 at night, and then I had to do my homework to be ready for school the next day. I would always be really tired. But I knew education is important to succeed in this country. I want to be a pediatrician. For that I have to go to school and work hard. Many times I sat in my room crying. I asked, "Why God? Why did this happen to me? I haven't done anything wrong to deserve this."

In April 2009, I heard about this wonderful person named Melanie Carey, pastor at First United Methodist Church in Ypsilanti. I got in touch with her. She supported me in any way possible. The church helped me financially in driving to school and many other things. When the congregation heard about my frequent weekends going without food, a group set up a weekly rotation to provide groceries. When I ultimately lost the cleaning job, a member found me a clerical position at a cemetery.

This church and many other people from a parenting small group helped me get a flight to Guatemala to visit my parents. I went to see them one year after our big tragedy. We spent Christmas and New Year's together.

The First United Methodist Church in Ypsilanti was a big help for me. I really appreciate the members' help. Without their support I wouldn't be able to share my story. When Melanie and her husband realized how much I missed my own family, they took me into their home for my senior year. This stable family life produced positive results. I worked fewer hours, studied more, and improved my grades, which had begun to fall markedly.

Before I met Melanie, I had a very difficult time. There would be days that I wouldn't eat because I had no money. But since I found this church, which I have joined, I have been able to do so many things, such as graduate from high school and be published in a national magazine (*New World Outlook*). I had the opportunity to do these things because the members of First United Methodist Church helped me so much.

It makes a big difference to have people there for you who are willing to help. Without all of them, I would've been just another student who dropped out of school to support herself. I thank them so much for their help. Melanie says it takes a village to raise a kid, and I found such a village here.

Their support has changed my life for good. I actually have a future. I hosted a graduation open house and invited everyone at the church to attend. I graduated because of my church family. I have been truly blessed by God, who put all of them in my way.

Faith is the only thing I had. And my faith helped me face all the challenges that I have encountered. I am so grateful that God put all of these people in my way. I am so thankful. I hope we can help other families not to get separated like my family did.

About the Author

Joan M. Maruskin is a United Methodist minister with the Susquehanna Conference in South Central Pennsylvania. She is in extension ministry as the National Administrator of the Church World Service Immigration and Refugee Program (CWSIRP) Religious Services Program, which provides spiritual care to immigrant detainees of all faiths in government-run immigration detention centers. She previously worked with CWSIRP as its Washington representative, advocating for immigrants, refugees, migrants, and asylum seekers and served as the executive director of the York County Council of Churches in York, Pennsylvania. She founded the People of the Golden Vision, an interfaith immigrants' rights group. She is presently a member of the advisory board for Church World Service of Lancaster, Pennsylvania, and on the Salem Square Neighborhood Association Board in York. She has a bachelor's degree in education from California State University (PA) and a master's degree in education from Johns Hopkins University and is a graduate of Wesley Theological Seminary, where she earned her MDiv and DMin in race, ethnicity, and the Wesleyan perspective. Ms. Maruskin lives in York, has two sons, and is the grandmother of six grandsons and one granddaughter.

Further Reading

La Biblia y la Inmigración: Guía para una Bienvenida Radical
por Joan M. Maruskin
Immigration and the Bible: A Guide for Radical Welcome (Spanish translation)
ISBN: 978-0-9848177-3-3
M3131-2012-01
$7.00

[이민과 성경: 철저하고 적극적인 환대를 위한 지침서]
Immigration and the Bible: A Guide for Radical Welcome (Korean)
by Joan M. Maruskin
ISBN: 978-0-9848177-4-0
M3132-2012-01
$7.00

response magazine, April 2012 issue, focusing on immigration

Available from Mission Resource Center
1-800-305-9857
www.missionresourcecenter.org

Immigration and the Bible website:
www.unitedmethodistwomen.org/immigrationstudy